Praise ⦀⦀⦀⦀⦀⦀⦀⦀⦀⦀⦀⦀⦀⦀

Jesus in the Wt

G000080568

"Gina Messina takes the hot button political issues of our time and weaves them together with partisan talking points and actual Biblical stories and admonitions. This refreshing take on contemporary American struggles gives the best clear-eyed call to be Christian that I've read. This is a needed antidote to current anguish."
- Sr. Simone Campbell, Nuns on the Bus

"Journalists in America: stop asking Jerry Falwell Jr., Pat Robertson, Robert Jeffress, and Franklin Graham to represent Christianity in the political realm. Instead, ask Gina Messina, author of Jesus in the White House. Her new book is delightfully written with both theological and political savvy. The voice you've been waiting for. Highly recommended!"
- Brian D. McLaren, Author of The Great Spiritual Migration

"Scholarship with a cheeky edge. Serious questions served with a side of humor. And Jesus in the West Wing. Gina Messina considers intriguing possibilities for a new politics."
- Tom Roberts, National Catholic Reporter

"As someone sentenced to Russian labour camps for singing a song in a church, I have experienced a society that claims to worship Christ but does not live out the teachings of Jesus. I've seen how the Bible has been used hypocritically to justify conservative oligarchic political order with the goal of extracting money from the people and make the poor people poorer. Jesus is an anarchist and revolutionary, I say. And that's why Gina Messina's book should be on the "must-read" shelf."
- Nadya Tolokonnikova, Pussy Riot

"The data on how different categories of Christians voted in the 2016 Presidential election are frankly baffling. Gina Messina unpacks the issues in a cogent way in her book. My hope is that what seems so obvious - that the example of Jesus calls all Christians to care about divisions and suffering and to act on it - will, as Gina presents the case, spark some soul searching and genuine debate and action."

- Katherine Marshall, Ph.D., Berkley Center for Religion, Peace, and World Affairs

"A new work by clearly one of the most creative scholars in the US today. Messina continues to explore the impact of religion in public life here in the US, and especially how it affects the lives of women. In Jesus in the White House: Make Humanity Great Again, she clearly demonstrates that so many policies of the country that boast a wall of separation between church and state (Jefferson) are now governed by an administration whose policies are crafted by a distortion of Christian teaching, which curiously the majority of both Catholic and Evangelical voters find appealing. A must read for anyone who wants to understand the state of the political question in the US today."

- Don C. Benjamin, Ph.D., Arizona State University

JESUS IN THE WHITE HOUSE

Make Humanity Great Again

JESUS IN THE WHITE HOUSE

Gina Messina

Published by The FAR Press
An imprint of Blaise Publications
Cleveland, Ohio

www.thefarpress.com

Printed in the United States of America

Library of Congress Cataloging-in-Publication-Data

Name: Messina, Gina author.
Title: Jesus in the White House: Make Humanity Great Again
Description: Cleveland: The FAR Press [2017]

Identifiers: LCCN 2017909474 | ISBN 9780998967516

DEDICATION

For my dad Biagio and my grandfather Edward

Contents

Acknowledgments

Writing a book, like every part of life, is a communal act. This book would have never come to fruition if it were not for the amazing people I have in my life and to whom I owe my deep gratitude. First, I would like to thank Steve Mazan, a brilliant comic and dear friend who read the manuscript and added his humor to help lift the tone of the book. Also, I am so grateful for Joe Laguardia, who wrote a quick-witted foreword and always gives critical advice. I continually benefit from his wisdom and am thankful for his kinship.

To my wonderful community of women to whom I turn for support; they are my life-long colleagues and friends who give me encouragement and love, and are always willing to read my "shitty first draft." Especially Jennifer Zobair, Xochitl Alvizo, Caroline Kline, and Elise Edwards.

I am particularly grateful to Carrie, Lori, and my "favorite" Uncle Basil for taking an interest in my work, even when we disagree. And to my brothers Biagio and Tony who always take my early morning and late night calls to offer advice and help me get re-centered.

It is my dad, Biagio, who keeps me on my toes when discussing politics. We have Sunday family dinner at my house nearly every week. My dad, who moved from Sicily to the U.S. when he was just five years old, has a lot to say about the state of American politics, but has never voted. Every week we banter back and forth. My dad always takes the opposite side from me. I admit there are moments when I become frustrated, but most of the time I see the dissension as practice that helps me to sort out my ideas and articulate them clearly.

My dad is my best friend. There is no one in the world to whom I am closer. He is a jokester and my daughter always says that the best part of Grandpa is his personality. That warms my heart and it is true. While he is generally wrong on his political views (I imagine him rolling his eyes right now reading this), my dad has a big heart and goes out of his way to help anyone. He's the favorite uncle, the grandpa all the grandkids are excited to see, and the loyal friend that keeps you in stitches. Whenever I'm with my dad I am smiling because that is the kind of person he is.

I always say I am my father's daughter and I am proud of that. We often think differently, but my work ethic, sense of commitment to serve, and belief in social justice come from what I've learned from him. I tell my dad I hope to run for office one day and he tells me if I do, he will register and vote for the first time…so he can vote against me. I am pretty sure he is kidding.

Finally, and most important of all in this long litany of thanks, I am deeply grateful for my smart, funny, and delightful daughter, Sarah. She sometimes gives up time with me so I can write and is always enthusiastic to help me through the process. She has taught me about love, has given me strength, and is the very best part of my life.

Foreword

"Why Would Jesus *Want* to Run for President?"

by Joseph LaGuardia

Why would Jesus even *want* to run for President. If he did, the birther people would have a field day, waving the Gospel of Luke around as if it were a birth certificate. Then the capitalists would comb the gospels seeking more and more information to show that Jesus was a socialist, not a capitalist. Finally, people of faith would be up in arms, since becoming president would seem to be the opposite of everything Jesus stood for.

The nay-sayers would dump a bucket of quotes at his feet, wouldn't they, daring him to spin them into a reasonable facsimile of a candidate's profile? The Beatitudes would be first, I think, followed closely by his injunction to "wash one another's feet." Then there'd be his admonitions that the last should be first and the first last, and to become like little children and go after the lost sheep and forgive everyone and take the last place at a banquet and turn the other cheek and give away your cloak and the quotation bucket would still be half full.

His stunt in the temple with the money changers would outrage the pharmacy maker who turned a thirteen dollar pill into a $750 pill as if it were a brilliant thing to do in a capitalist culture. People would gnash their teeth at the company he kept, not to mention his refusal to send armies of angels to avenge attacks on his person. Which companies would exercise their right under Citizens United to fund his campaign? His request to go sell all that you have and give the proceeds to the poor would be extremely offensive to the majority of stakeholders. There would be nothing left to trickle down! Is this a man we would want for President?

But then, we are considering the role of president as we have seen that office filled and fulfilled during our lifetime in these United States. Might there be another way of looking at it? Would there be a way to modify that job description so that Jesus would *want* to throw his hat, if he wore one, into the ring?

Maybe. After all, this is the One with a capital "O" who did not consider being God a thing to be clung to, but emptied himself and took the form of a servant. In fact, he modeled those suffering servant passages in Isaiah. He was the Word, the Explanation, the Son of God, and he became flesh. Plunk. He plunked himself into our messy, earthy existence. I wonder if he screamed when he was teething.

Pope Francis is giving us an example of a world leader who is re-writing the role of pope. How would Jesus re-define himself as president? He would be peaceful, right? He would know what it's like to be human, sometimes cold, thirsty, hungry, without a roof over his head. He could continue his obvious penchant for rubbing shoulders with the poor, the unhealthy, the marginalized. He would model for us how to meet and relate to someone with a different sexuality, a different religion, or a different social status.

As the Franciscan sister, Ilia Delio wrote: "Jesus taught us that salvation is about whole-making and healing," she continues, "It's not this grace of being rescued from a depraved, fallen world. It's that grace of love that heals us. I think that's what it means to be saved: to be healed and to be whole and to be sent on our way to be whole-makers ourselves."

Salvation. Salus, Healing. What if a whole presidential term were about "healing?" Or, better, what if Ilia Delio is correct in echoing Teilhard de Chardin, and President Jesus would — in human form — be moving all of creation to its evolutionary conclusion, which Teilhard calls "The Omega Point?"

Teilhard developed the concept of evolutionary Christianity, theorizing that the whole of creation was progressing toward fulfillment in Christ. The goal of the universe, which he called the Omega Point, was full consciousness with God.

"He believed that love energy was at the heart of the Big Bang," she says. "As love emerges in evolution, there is a rise in consciousness."[1]

Believers already hold that the Spirit of Jesus is present in so many individuals and communities, and this Holy Spirit is engaged in this evolutionary effort described by Delio. But how much it would mean to those of us who have weaker faith and need concrete, sensory experiences, to have another incarnation of Jesus, this time as a world leader!

But would Jesus want to go through all this again? He would know full well that his policies, his words, and above all, his actions would be unacceptable. People would be scandalized that his lifestyle was not at all befitting a world leader. "He's acting like a servant," they would say. Congress would remain divided about him. Some would say he forfeited any kind of respect by his coddling of the poor and those whom our economic systems have forced to the lowest tier.

But I think he would want to be president if he could count on a huge majority of us humans to support his campaign and multiply his actions. Because once you limit yourself by taking on a particular form and being in a particular place, even the best media coverage in the world cannot bring about the reforms you cherish and find necessary. Reincarnation is not all it's cracked up to be!

One reason I can think of that Jesus would *not* want to be president is his comment that even if someone rises from

---

1 Jamie Manson, "The Evolution of Ilia Delio," *The National Catholic Reporter*, July 16, 2014.

the dead, the naysayers will not believe in what he is saying and doing. And that's why he sent his followers to enflesh his work, to be his priests (or presidents, if you will) in the world, to translate what he modeled into their own spheres, their own messy lives.

Unfortunately, following him, continuing what he started, associating with the same kind of people, keeping in mind the poor, the widows and orphans at the edges of our societies—all these things are *not* a walk in the park. They are often thankless tasks, earning us not points but trouble. We may end up being crucified like he was.

And so if Jesus does not run for president, it may be our hat we see in the ring.

Preface

Everything I've learned about being a patriot, I learned from my grandfather. He was a marine, a WWII veteran who served at Pearl Harbor just after the attack. He had seen things, experienced things I could never possibly imagine. After returning from war, he married, had children, and became a steel worker in my hometown of Cleveland, Ohio.

His employer was Republican Steel, eventually becoming LTV Steel. It was hard work, but respectable work. He was grateful for his job and the life it afforded him and his family. He was the working middle class achieving the American Dream.

Grandpa loved his country and was proud that he had served. He believed in American values; freedom of speech was especially important to him, and he thought jury duty was a privilege. In fact, it angered him that many whined about being called to serve in court. He argued that we live in a nation with rights and privileges for which others have died. As he saw it, being invited to serve our government in any way — to be a part of a jury of our peers — we should greet with gratitude, not annoyance - or disrespect.

He was a life-long Democrat and was proud of his political affiliation. My grandfather thought of the Democratic party as the party of the working man. It was the party that stood for the rights of the middle class and those who were struggling in poverty. Having grown up in a household where his mother scrounged for vegetables in garbage cans to make soup for her children each night, my grandfather knew what it was like to be hungry. His political affiliation was personal and he only voted for candidates who supported his values. The Democratic party stood for economic justice, union rights, healthcare, and serving the needs of all the nation's people.

He donated to the party regularly and my first real memory of him talking politics was when Walter Mondale ran against Ronald Reagan in 1984. I was nine years old. I always knew we were a family of Democrats. I didn't quite know what that meant, but I knew were were voting for Mondale. Sad to say that I remember thinking there was no way Mondale could win because he chose a woman as his running mate. Now, I cringe at the way patriarchy had dominated my thinking and Geraldine Ferraro is a personal heroine.

When I turned eighteen, I was excited to register to vote. In fact, I found it surprising that anyone would not do the same - especially to avoid jury duty (something I hear often). I voted in my first election in 1996 and voted for Bill Clinton. Yet, at such a young age, I knew little about the issues and voted based on family influence. It wasn't until I was in my mid-twenties that I recognized the responsibility that came with voting, and my feminist progressive self was birthed.

Grandpa always told me that politics is about the issues. You attack issues, not people — a life lesson I never forget, although admittedly I sometimes fail. Like my grandfather, I am a Democrat at heart. My political commitments are grounded in a family tradition of patriotism and commitment to the American Dream. Likewise, my Catholic upbringing and feminist ideals also inform my stances on social policy.

Inspired by Catholic social teaching, social justice is critical to me when I consider political issues. I ask myself: Who will benefit and who will suffer? Is my stance about me as an individual or about our larger community? How would Jesus respond to my vote? I have often thought about how Jesus might respond to our political culture in the U.S. Now, with President Donald J. Trump elected by 81 percent of Evangelicals and 65 percent of Catholics, I wonder what Jesus would say about the role that our faith plays in our politics and voting patterns.

We Christians claim Jesus as a guiding force in our political decisions, but we do so without knowing who Jesus really was. As a result, our votes often do not represent the teachings of Jesus. And so, I write this book with the intention of exploring the historical Jesus, his politics, and how a Jesus campaign would unfold in the twenty-first century. I also examine how twenty-first century Christians would react to the foundational messages of Jesus applied to our social policy. Many who invoke Jesus' name — and voted for Trump — may be surprised to find out that he is not the Jesus they thought.

If Jesus Ran for President

The greatest need today is for Christians who are active and critical, who don't accept situations without analyzing them inwardly and deeply.

- Archbishop Oscar Romero

If Jesus ran for president, what would his campaign look like? Where would he stand on social policy? And who would (not) vote for him? With our current political dialogue dominated by supposed Christian views and a nation that overwhelmingly claims the teachings of Jesus as the basis for its morality, what would the response be if we came face to face with the (unintentional) founder of the tradition? How would we respond to Jesus teaching us today? And how would Jesus respond to us?

In a nation where the majority of Evangelical and Catholic populations elected Donald J. Trump to the highest office in the land, many people are left scratching their heads and wondering how Jesus' teachings could result in a leader of the free world who has mocked the disabled, sexually assaulted women, and openly made racist and xenophobic statements. Likewise, his immediate acts as POTUS are in direct conflict with Christianity. Banning Muslims, dismantling the Affordable Care Act, building a wall to exclude immigrants, and single-handedly destroying international relationships are acts that do not fit at all with Jesus' teachings of inclusion, love, social justice, and liberation.

When I began writing this book there were seventeen Republican and five Democratic candidates. The Fox News Republican debate in my hometown of Cleveland kicked me into high gear. What stood out to me the most, other than Donald Trump's continuous insults and poor treatment of journalist Megyn Kelly, was that every candidate brought God into their responses. Jesus' name was regularly invoked and the candidates' Christian views heavily impacted their positions on social policy.

It was one of the only times Fox News graced my television screen. I am a feminist, a Catholic theologian, and a progressive liberal. I am a registered independent, but have only ever voted for Democratic candidates. I volunteered for Hilary Clinton's campaign in 2008 and again in 2016. I think Barack Obama was the greatest president of my generation, and I definitely "feel the Bern."

Before this election, I rarely watched Republican debates, although surely God was a regular topic before now. The use of God to justify gun rights, anti-immigration legislation, homophobic laws, and the denial of women's human rights along with the incessant mention of Jesus seems fodder in the Republican arena.

Trump became a Presbyterian when he decided to run for office. Although he could not name a single biblical verse when asked, he claims it was his faith that led him to embrace a "pro-life" stance. According to former presidential candidate Marco Rubio, it is Judeo-Christian values that make America special, and his faith influences his every decision. And Ted Cruz claims God talks to him every day and is the force that leads him in his anti-woman, anti-LGBTQIA position. It's easy to imagine Jesus telling Cruz that it's not God he's been talking to - maybe he's being catfished.

During the 2016 election cycle, Trump's primary talking point was that he was the last chance for the Republican Party and conservative white Christians to reclaim their power and their country. Trump argued,

> If we don't win this election, you'll never see another Republican and you'll have a whole different church structure...I think this will be the last election that the Republicans have a chance of winning because you're going to have people flowing across the border, you're going to have illegal immigrants coming in and they're going to be legalized and they're going to be able to vote, and once that all happens you can forget it.[1]

Former House Republican Michele Bachmann and evangelical advisor to Trump, echoed his claims saying, "this is the

---

1 Donald J. Trump, "Interview with Pat Robertson," *Christian Broadcasting Network*, September 9, 2016. Television.

last election when we have a chance to vote for somebody who will stand up for godly moral principles. This is it."[2]

Jesus, who happened to be a refugee, was not a nationalist. He did not believe in excluding people based on any qualifying factor. Our use of nationalism has created an interpretation of God as a "state-sponsored deity" who offers justification for us to hate those whom we view as "un-American."[3] Though such ideas are in direct contrast to the teachings of Jesus, Christianity is used as the foundation for such arguments.

On the other side, Democratic candidates rarely acknowledge God and religion and few if any claim that their stances on social policy are shaped by religion. For instance, recall Vice President Joe Biden during the 2012 election cycle acknowledging his Catholic faith and stance on abortion; and then acknowledging that his religious beliefs have no bearing on his politics and should not be forced upon others.[4]

The U.S. is a secular nation, and yet, religion regularly enters the political arena for Republicans. Stances on issues that are oppressive particularly for women, Latinos, African Americans, and the LGBTQIA community are justified as being ordained by God. And while the U.S. claims religious freedom,

---

2 Michele Bachmann, "The Brody File," *Christian Broadcasting Network,* September 1, 2016. Television.

3 Stephen Mattson, "When Christians Love Political Power More Than People," *Sojourners,* June 20, 2017. Retrieved from https://sojo.net/articles/when-christians-love-political-power-more-people.

4 Amy Davidson, "The Abortion Debate: Biden's Faith, Ryan's Extremism," *The New Yorker,* October 12, 2012. Retrieved from http://www.newyorker.com/news/amy-davidson/the-abortion-debate-bidens-faith-ryans-extremism.

social policy is proposed and implemented based on Christian ideals. Such actions deny citizens the right to make their own choices based on their own religious values and identities. Jesus would not agree with any of this given that those who sat at his table were "the least of these."

Imagine Jesus being in the U.S. today and launching a bid for the White House. Don't imagine him announcing his candidacy on the deck of an aircraft carrier — he's more of a homeless shelter guy. Would he be the conservative "Christian" the right often labels him? Would he be a Democrat as so many book titles have claimed? How do his teachings measure up with the various political parties, and would there be room for Jesus at any of their tables?

If Jesus ran for president, he would not be a Republican...or a Democrat. Both parties want to claim the Christian founder as their own mascot, but Jesus would be anti-establishment. Not like Donald Trump, like Caesar Chavez.

As an independent candidate, I imagine Jesus would develop his campaign around his core teachings of love, inclusion, liberation, and social justice. A message centered on such principles is in direct contrast to the GOP's stance on marriage equality, women's rights, immigration reform, and so on. Conservatism continues to ignore the structural injustices that pervade our nation. As Jim Wallis notes, "to call for individual self-improvement and a return to family values while ignoring the pernicious effects of poverty, racism, and sexism is to continue blaming the victim."[5]

While Democrats are referred to as the "left," most see themselves as moderate and are working the party lines to be favorable to red and blue voters. Likewise, liberals often lack the link between personal responsibility and social transformation that is needed for positive change.[6] Jesus would never apologize for his radical perspective and would stand firm in his beliefs at any cost — another fact well demonstrated in the Gospels and by Jesus' eventual crucifixion. There are few people today who would give their lives for their beliefs and most politicians won't take a stand based on their faith for fear of losing an election.

Can you imagine the attack ads on presidential candidate Jesus? The Gospels once revered as guides on how to live our lives would become weapons to keep Jesus out of the oval office.

> *"Jesus is a socialist!"*
> *"Where's his birth certificate?"*
> *"Believes in free healthcare!"*
> *"Caught with a prostitute!"*

I appreciate Bill Maher's bit on why Jesus could never be on the Republican ticket.

> Feed the hungry? That sounds suspiciously like welfare.
> Heal the sick?...For free? That is definitely Obamacare.

---

5 Jim Wallis, *The Soul of Politics: Beyond the Religious Right and Secular Left* (New York: Harcourt Brace & Company), 1995, xv.
6 Ibid.

Turn the other cheek? Maybe you didn't hear, Jesus, but this is the party that cheers executions.[7]

Maher goes on to offer a satirical timeline for Jesus' campaign that leaves him in the back of the pack by day ten after his "book" is labeled "troubling," and he is attacked for being anti-business, Jewish, and pro-union given his career as a carpenter.[8]

We have adopted Jesus as an American icon, and in doing so have twisted his words and teachings to support our own ideas. It's enough to make one think that those WWJD bumper stickers stand for *"What Wouldn't Jesus Do?"* And so, if Jesus did run for president, regardless of being in a country that has adopted him as its icon and claims a Christian identity, Jesus would never be elected. His understanding, loving approach would probably bar him from even getting a reality show—which appears to be key for a presidential resume these days.

That's right. Likely no Christian would vote for Jesus and most would attack him for his teachings and politics. While some may find this surprising, Jesus was indeed highly political. Some might like his message, but the media would label him unelectable and the GOP would go after him for being a left wing, pro-union, welfare supporting, Obamacare enthusiast. Others would argue that Jesus is a nice guy, but doesn't know a thing about running a country. If it came down to it, and the country were under threat, Jesus would never push the

---

7 "Episode 226," *Real Time with Bill Maher, Home Box Office,* HBO, Los Angeles, CA. September 30, 2011. Television.
    8 Ibid.

red button. Instead, Republicans would rather him be a mascot for their campaigns — "Jesus the Carpenter" — perhaps like "Joe the Plumber."

As citizens in a democracy with the opportunity to vote, we claim Jesus as a guiding force in our decisions, but we do so without knowing who Jesus really was. Many who invoke Jesus' name — and voted for Trump — may be surprised to find out that he is not the Jesus they thought. While Jesus the American Icon might have a chance in a presidential election, Jesus the Jewish carpenter of the Gospels would be laughed off the ballot. Given that his name is continually invoked in political campaigns and speeches, it is important to explore what Jesus' values were, how they apply to our current social policy, and why his politics would not be supported today.

If Jesus were in the White House the stature of American politics would be a far cry from what currently divides the nation. In the pages that follow, I offer a portrait of who the historical Jesus was, layout his political stances based on his teachings, and relate them to contemporary issues that are dominating our political terrain.

I will try and lay out these arguments, and point out the hypocrisies with the grace, kindness, and love that Jesus would. But I admit, I am often guilty of falling short of his teachings...

The Real Jesus
Revealed

> Social justice is a Christian tradition, not a liberal agenda.
>   - Stephen Mattson

We all think we know who the real Jesus was. Regardless of our religious traditions, we have been introduced to him one way or another: *A Charlie Brown Christmas, Jesus Christ Superstar, The Passion, The DaVinci Code,* etc. And yet, most of us have no idea who the historical Jesus was. Many of us have been so blinded by the versions of Jesus we have come to know, either through an interpretation of the Bible, church, or Hollywood, that we've never taken the time to find out who he really was or how his true mission relates to our lives today.

To begin with, Jesus was not a good Catholic (*gasp*); he was a Jew, born in modern day Palestine. He did not look like the "Hollywood Jesus" we have come to know in America - no blond hair or blue eyes. He was a Middle Eastern man with a dark complexion who resembled the population so many people unreasonably fear today. Basically, he'd have a tough time getting through our U.S. airports.

Jesus was a radical. He was born into the marginalized peasant class and came from the highly oppressed Galilee, an area that was undergoing rapid social change. His hometown of Nazareth was just a few miles from the political center for King Herod. This gave Jesus a very distinct perspective on the disparity between the wealthy and impoverished within his community and culture. His teachings throughout the Gospels demonstrate this perspective and are focused on care for the poor and marginalized. Not care with co-pays and qualifications to see if the needy had pre-existing conditions — just care.

Because of his own personal experience Jesus challenged both government and religion for their oppression of the "least of these." His ministry called people to leave behind their belongings and follow him. Jesus stood with the poorest of the poor, the tax collectors and prostitutes; he cared for the lepers, and believe it or not, had women disciples. Jesus was a liberator. He called for the uprooting of oppression wherever it existed - across all boundaries and with no exceptions.

Compassion was a critical part of his message. In Luke 6:36 he calls us to "Be compassionate as God is compassionate;" to bring together the qualities of God and the way we lead our lives. To be compassionate means to show concern for others. If we expand on that idea, it means to nurture, care, give and support life, to be empathetic and loving. This is how Jesus understood God, and thus how he calls us to live as individuals and in our communities.

Marcus Borg sheds light on this, explaining that Jesus understood compassion as both an individual virtue and a sociopolitical paradigm. Community should embody compassion; and this vision was realized within his movement.[1]

Being the radical that he was, Jesus continually challenged dominant sociopolitical structures of his time by calling for a change in the way people engaged one another, and a change in the way the government and religion responded to the needs of the people. For Jesus, compassion was political. He identified it as the fundamental basis for developing value for community. Nonetheless, Sarah Palin would probably mock Jesus for being a "community organizer."

Jesus the American Icon

The historical Jesus is quite different from Jesus the American Icon. As Stephen Prothero explains, "Jesus has stood not on some unchanging rock of ages, but on the shifting sands of economic circumstances, political calculations, and cultural trends."[2] Within our culture and our lives we have conceived a

1 Marcus J. Borg, *Meeting Jesus Again for the First Time: The Historical Jesus and the Heart of Contemporary Faith* (New York: HarperSanFransico, 1994), 47.

2 Stephen Prothero, *American Jesus: How the Son of God Became a National Icon* (New York: Farrar, Straus, and Giroux, 2003), 8.

Jesus who mirrors our own "hopes and fears...[a] reflection of [ourselves] and our nation."[3]

Throughout American history, we have imagined Jesus in many ways that ignore his true cultural heritage. From the "Hollywood Jesus" and extending to representations of multiple identities of different groups who have adopted an image of Jesus to represent their beliefs. I personally think he would object to the Klansman representation, but alas, the KKK has also claimed Jesus as their own. Interesting, considering that Jesus was a Jew. That said, the KKK grand dragon was stunned when told that Jesus was not white. He responded, "I don't know what he was."[4] Exactly my point.

Remember, Jesus called his followers to give their belongings to the poor, to live a lifestyle that rejects materialism — a teaching in direct contrast with the lives many of us lead in American culture. Let me say upfront, I am guilty. I have an unhealthy obsession with handbags, and little makes me happier than a sale at Nordstrom. I own it. But that doesn't change who Jesus was or his teachings. Even if he was alive today I don't think Jesus would be swayed by Nordstrom—-although I have seen amazing sandals there. Rather, he was making a particular statement with such a calling — reject society as we know it and embrace compassion and community.

---

3 Ibid., 9.

4 Marie Brownie, "See Ku Klux Klan Grand Dragon's stunned reaction after interviewer tells him Jesus was not white." *Christianity Today*. July 2, 2014. Retrieved from http://www.christiantoday.com/article/see.ku.klux.klan.grand.dragons.stunned.reaction.after.interviewer.tells.him.jesus.was.not.white.video/38560.htm.

We want Jesus to be a middle class American living in the suburbs who likes to drink Starbucks (full disclosure I expect he'd be a "tall, mild roast, fair trade" guy—you know, simple). We want a Jesus who embraces our "Christian spin on the American dream,"[5] a Jesus who looks like us. That is the Jesus we would be most comfortable with.

And so, it makes sense that we become confused about who Jesus really was – we cannot imagine what it would mean for him to live today and take a stand because we have been overly focused on creating a Jesus that mirrors ourselves and in some cases, on adopting him as a mascot. For instance, the "Buddy Jesus" of the cult classic film *Dogma* (1999) so perfectly encapsulates our efforts to make Jesus who we want him to be, rather than who he really was.

A quick look at the Bible and we see the image of a simple carpenter calling his community to stand together, feed the poor, reject religious and governmental norms, and work for peace and justice. Jesus wanted every person to have his or her fair share and to be liberated from all oppressions. Can't you just hear Donald Trump calling him "weak," "clueless," "unbalanced?" No doubt, he would find the idea of a fair share ludicrous and would demand that Jesus read his book, *The Art of Making the Deal.*

The Politics of Jesus

---

5 David Platt, *Radical: Taking Back Your Faith from the American Dream* (Colorado Springs, CO: Multnomah Books, 2010), 13.

To argue that Jesus was not political is to disregard everything he stood for. While many people claim that Jesus was focused solely on individual morality, in fact, Jesus called for a restructuring of the entire socio-political terrain of his time. We cannot forget that Jesus lived in a highly politicized culture. During the first century, Israel was occupied by Rome. Jews were treated very poorly and poverty was widespread. The Roman Empire wielded its power over Israel and its people by holding public crucifixions for anyone who rebelled against the government.

Because we regularly see images of Jesus on the cross, we have become desensitized to what crucifixion is — an extreme form of torture and execution that keeps its victims lingering for up to two weeks. The Romans intentionally crucified these individuals along the most crowded streets to strike terror into the community and remind the already oppressed to remain silent and accept their powerlessness.

This Roman colonial occupation of Israel played a significant role in shaping Jesus' politics. According to Obery Hendricks Jr., the brutality and pervasiveness of suffering inflicted on the Jewish people by the Romans had a clear impact on the political consciousness and social witness of Jesus.[6] Although Christians refer to Jesus as the Son of God, during his lifetime he was an oppressed Jew subjected to the cruelty of the Roman Empire. And so, oppression was a critical issue for Jesus and it is a significant theme throughout his teachings in

6 Obery Hendricks Jr., *The Politics of Jesus: Rediscovering the True Revolutionary Nature of the Teachings of Jesus and How They have been Corrupted* (New York: Doubleday, 2006), 55.

the Gospels.

While we recognize Jesus as the founder of the Christian tradition, this was not his intent. As Hendricks points out, Jesus did not write doctrine, he did not establish a church, nor did he endorse a religious hierarchy.[7] Jesus created a political movement, one that called for loving our neighbors as we love ourselves. His disciples were not just his followers, but his partners in his movement. Jesus understood that hierarchy does not work. Partners within movements bring different strengths and all need to be celebrated. Although Jesus led the movement, every person's efforts counted and no person was more important than another. Together they challenged the marginalization, brutality, and poverty forced upon those not favored by the Roman government. The Gospels offer insight into the ways in which both Jesus and his followers challenged oppressors through action, prayer, and narrative.

A Virgin Birth?

Beginning with the virgin birth, the Gospel writers were making a strong statement about Jesus' politics. And by the way, the Gospels were not written by the apostles. They were written long after their deaths. However, the message of Jesus lived on and was strong. So the scribes who did write the Gospels knew that writing a fantastic narrative about Jesus' birth was critical. Way before movies and comic books, writers knew a strong "origin story" was important.

---

7 Ibid.

Tales of virgin births are not uncommon. I will never forget my own realization of this when one of my graduate school professors (who happened to be an Episcopal priest) informed me that "virgin births are a dime a dozen." It was my first awakening to what we can really know about Jesus and, like many people who hear this for the first time, I was astounded. But it is true; The Buddha, Lao Tzu, Alexander the Great and most importantly here, Julius Caesar are among those who have been recorded as being virgin births. The intent of such a story is to demonstrate the greatness of a person; that his or her life was so critical in the shaping of our world it was foretold in birth.[8] Knowing this now, I'm surprised Donald Trump hasn't claimed to be a virgin birth. "I just came out. It was tremendous. Everyone loved it."

The infancy narratives of Jesus appear only in Matthew and Luke. Both have particular perspectives based on their cultural attitudes; Matthew is Jewish and Luke is Gentile. We are familiar with the story of Jesus' birth; however, what we don't realize is that we have mashed together two stories and have ignored features of both. For instance, in Luke, the angel appears to Mary, but he appears to Joseph in Matthew. Jesus was born in a manger in Bethlehem in Luke, but at home in Nazareth in Matthew. The wise men appear in Matthew and the shepherds in Luke.[9]

---

8 See Margaret Nutting Ralph, *And God Said What? An Introduction to Biblical Literary Forms* (Mahwah, New Jersey: Paulist Press, 2003).

9 For more on the differences between Matthew and Luke's infancy narratives, see Nutting Ralph. Also see Raymond Brown, *The Birth of the Messiah: A Commentary on the Infancy Narratives in the Gospels of Matthew and Luke* (New York: Doubleday, 1993); and Jane Schaberg., *The Illegitimacy of Jesus: A Feminist Theological Interpretation of the Narratives* (New York: HarperCollins, 1986).

If Jesus was not a virgin birth, this question natural-
ly follows: who was his father? That was the first question I
asked my professor. His response? With a boisterous belly laugh
he blurted out, "How would I know?!" Truth be told, it can't
be said for certain. Some argue that Joseph actually fathered
Jesus and others claim that Mary was raped by a Roman soldier
named Pantera[10] (Yes, that is where the heavy metal band got its
name).

The point is that both of these stories were written well
after the death of Jesus, in about 80CE, and with intent and
from particular perspectives. First, they sought to demonstrate
that Jesus was an extraordinary person who walked the earth,
which is the objective of an infancy narrative or virgin birth
story. And second, they put Jesus on the same level as Caesar,
the man who claimed to be a virgin birth, who demanded that
his name be hallowed, and who commanded the colonization of
Israel and the brutalization of Jews. Such a statement is highly
political and continues the radical nature of Jesus' actions within his ministry.

A Revolutionary Baptism

Jesus' decision to be baptized in the Jordan River by John the
Baptist was not random, nor was it because John was his cous-
in. Rather, Jesus was taking a revolutionary stance against the
Roman government. Water was readily available within the
confines of the land ruled by Caesar. However, John Dominic
Crossan explains, "a TransJordanian desert location and a bap-

10 See Schaberg, *The Illegitimacy of Jesus.*

tism in the Jordan, precisely the Jordan, had overtones, explicit or implicit, of political subversion."[11]

Jesus intentionally chose to head to the wilderness to seek out John the Baptist, a known radical agitator — who, by the way, ended up being executed and having his head served on a platter (Matthew 14:10-11). By choosing such a baptism, Jesus was leaving behind his life as a marginalized Jew living under the oppressive regime that denied his humanity. As he was birthed from the waters of the Jordan River, Jesus reclaimed power and professed a new identity as liberated and liberator.

Our Father: A Radical Prayer

Jesus' politics are well demonstrated in the "Our Father" — also known as the Lord's prayer — recited daily by many Christians and central to church service worship. In Luke 11:1 Jesus' disciples ask him to teach them how to pray. In doing so, they were not literally asking how to pray; as observant Jews they prayed regularly. Rather, they were asking "What is it that we stand for? What is our purpose as we travel about, healing, teaching, being persecuted and sometimes pursued?"[12] They wanted to know what they should pray for. Jesus responded with a list of elements that have become the "Our Father" we recite today. According to Hendricks, this is not just "a microcosm of his teachings, it was a codification of his actions."[13]

---

11 John Dominic Crossan, *The Historical Jesus: The Life of Mediterranean Jewish Peasant* (New York: HarperSanFrancisco, 1991), 235.
12 Ibid., 102.
13 Ibid., 107.

In saying "our father" Jesus was making an important point: he was naming God as the father of everyone. Granted, when I am in mass at my conservative Catholic church, I say "Our Mother and Father" — both because I refuse to use only male language to talk about God and because I delight in the reaction I get from those around me in the pews. I think Jesus would be delighted too. That said, regardless of gendered language, we must understand this as an egalitarian statement by Jesus.

Next, Jesus calls us to pray "Hallow Your name." During that time, only Caesar's name was to be "hallowed" or sanctified. Thus, Jesus was making a clear and radical statement that opposed Caesar's rule and called God to demonstrate God's holiness. Jesus' political motivations continue in this prayer. Taking a clear stance, he states that we must pray for the Roman Empire's colonization to end so that a kingdom of liberation can take its place — "Your kingdom come, Your will be done." Likewise, "give us our daily bread" continues a prayer to end Caesar's rule and the Roman colonization of Israel. The Jews were impoverished and hungry — a direct result of the socio-political situation.

Although it has been translated as "forgive us our trespasses," in actuality Jesus said "release us from our debts."[14] He was acknowledging that the colonization by Rome could not continue without its oppressive system that "forced its subjects into debt and dispossession." As Hendricks explains, "Forgiving the debts of others means not only decrying the exploitive ways

---

14 See Hendricks, 101-112.

of commerce and empire, but also refusing to participate in them any longer."[15]

Through the "Our Father," Jesus taught his disciples how to pray and how to present the people's needs to God. According to Hendricks,

> [Jesus] made clear to them that using their strength, their gifts, their spiritual ministrations, to make this a just work was the most important service they could render to God. He taught them to serve God by making sure that everyone has enough daily bread, that everyone is free from economic violence and exploitation, that everyone is delivered from the clutches of unjust kingdoms, principalities, and powers. In this way Jesus showed that the salvation that his followers must strive for is the salvation for all.[16]

We have heard and recited this prayer so many times, we have become desensitized to its meaning and value. The "Our Father" calls for the liberation of those who have been subjected to oppressive rule. It is through this prayer — and through all of Jesus' teachings — that we see his mission to acknowledge that the needs of every person are holy.

Healing the Sick

The very fact that Jesus ministered to the sick, specifically those who were rejected by society — the lepers, the disabled, the mentally ill — has political implications. In reaching out to

---

15 Ibid., 105. For a more detailed discussion on the prayer "Our Father" and its political nature, see Hendricks, The Politics of Jesus.
16 Hendricks, 110-111.

these individuals, Jesus offered them the opportunity to reclaim power in their own lives. He welcomed them to his movement and embraced them without judgement. And without proof of insurance.

While many of us read these stories in the Gospels and believe that Jesus literally healed the sick, we must understand the true intent of these passages. Rather than curing illness, by welcoming those who had been rejected by society because of their ailments, Jesus healed by

> removing the personal and social stigmas of uncleanliness, isolation, and rejection associated with these conditions. He opened his arms and brought the sick and the handicapped back into the community from which they'd been excluded, making the world humanly habitable and hospitable again for them.[17]

These actions perpetuated the growing disdain for Jesus by the authorities; however, they also perpetuated his appeal to those who were disenfranchised. Loved and hated at the same time: he sure sounds like a political figure.

Prophet and Teacher

Critical to understanding the person of Jesus is understanding the title, "Son of God." It is not one Jesus applied to himself, at least in the Synoptic Gospels. It is a title chief priests used to mock him as he hung on the cross (Matthew 27:43). He does

---

17 Scott McLennan, *Jesus was a Liberal: Reclaiming Christianity for All* (New York: Palgrave Macmillan, 2009), 7. Also see John Dominic Crossan *Jesus: A Revolutionary Biography* (HarperSanFrancisco: San Francisco, 1994), 82.

use the title in John's Gospel, a gospel written from a different source than the Synoptics (Matthew, Mark, and Luke). Nonetheless, there the title is used in a specific way. Jesus speaks of others being sons and daughters of God: "Blessed are the peacemakers, for they shall be called children of God" (Matthew 5:9). Paul also states, "All who are led by the Spirit of God are children of God," (Romans, 8:14). And so, Jesus recognized himself as a child of God in the way all are who live out God's will.

Jesus often referred to himself as a prophet and others called him a prophet too. In reading the Gospels we see that his actions and teachings were prophet-like; he called on the Jewish people - as well as other nations - to recognize God's will and speak on God's behalf.[18] He was recognized as being filled with wisdom. His teachings were not orthodox, but instead challenging, subversive, and revolutionary. Jesus encouraged people to see the world in a new and radical way through his use of proverbs and parables. He called his followers to recognize that God wanted compassion and love at the center of a new social and ethical vision.[19]

Conclusion

Throughout his ministry, Jesus strategized to expose the brutality those in power committed against the oppressed. He was "a social critic and an agitator, a drop out from the social

---

18 See Jaroslav Pelikan, *Jesus Throughout the Centuries: His Place in the History of Culture* (Harper and Row: New York, 1985). Also see Mark 6:4, 6:15; Matthew 21:11, 21:46; Luke 4:24, 7:16, and 13:33.

19 McLennan, 8.

climb, and the spokesman of a counterculture."[20] He focused on bringing to voice those whom the powerful silenced, naming the evils that existed within the socio-political structure, and demonstrating through action how positive change is possible. And he did so while calling for non-violence, refusing to persecute others, but instead recognizing the humanity of every person — even the oppressors — something radical even by today's standards.

While some people want to claim that Jesus was not political, in fact he is "a model of radical political action."[21] So the question becomes not whether Jesus was political but how Jesus would respond today to the ongoing oppression dictated by government? Where would he stand on social policy, and how would we respond to his position?

---

20 John Howard Yoder, *The Politics of Jesus: Vicit Agnus Noster* (Grand Rapids, MI: William B. Eerdmans Publishing Company, 1994), 1.
    21 Ibid., 2.

Jesus and Social Policy

> Together we imagine a circle of compassion with no one standing outside of it.
> - Peggy O'Neill, S. C.

With whom would Jesus stand in the twenty-first century, and who would sit at his table? Would Donald Trump — who claims a Christian identity — want to sit at that table? If Leonardo Da Vinci were to paint the Last Supper today, who would be in the picture? Trump? How would Jesus respond to his stance on social policy?

Would Jesus fear Muslims and argue that anyone practicing Islam should be labeled and tracked or banned from entering the U.S.? Would Jesus ask to be removed from the Quran where he's praised as a prophet second only to Muhammad? He doesn't seem like the jealous type.

Would Jesus demand we deport every — or any — undocumented immigrant? Would he demand a wall be built to keep people out? Jesus believed in liberation and social justice — inclusion, not exclusion. He preached forgiveness, which sure sounds a lot like amnesty.

What would Jesus say about the current attack on Planned Parenthood and women's reproductive rights? What about women's rights in general? Or pay equality? Parental leave? Violence against women?

In a world where God-fearing Christians associate guns with Jesus and more mass shootings occurred in 2015 than days of the year, would Jesus demand access to an AK 47 to protect his home?

Today individualism has become synonymous with American life, and our political engagement reflects such a culture. A vote for Jesus would be a vote for a political order that centers on community and one without borders. Jesus believed in inclusion; he welcomed all to his table regardless of qualifying factors. With Trump demanding we label and track some of our citizens because of their religious beliefs and that we ban Muslims from immigrating to the U.S., we are far from being a collective identity that is committed to the care of the community.

Jesus called for a society where people are not oppressed, where everyone is treated fairly and recognized as being made in the image of God. He called his followers — and indeed everyone — to look past imposed rules that did not improve quality of life so that they could focus on what mattered. He asked that people follow the Golden Rule, that they treat others as they want to be treated. He said, "Do not judge," and argued that if we love God and love our neighbor, every person would live in a just world. According to Jesus, it is the poor, the meek, the righteous, and the persecuted that will inherit the kingdom of God — not those who exercise power over others. So how do Jesus' teachings apply to our world today? Who are the persecuted? And how are we following the gospels accordingly?

I often say we need a Church that responds to the times. During a conversation with Tavis Smiley, he told me he does not want a Church that changes with the times, but a Church that is firm in its faith and doesn't waiver.[1] And Smiley is correct. It is not about changing the teachings of the Gospels or Jesus' ministry; rather it is about understanding his message and how it applies to our lives in the twenty-first century.

Many of the issues that exist today were not factors in Jesus' time. Yet, that does not change the foundational message of Jesus. Looking at social policy today, I will therefore examine how his teachings apply to our political culture and how they are often misused.

---

1 See "The Future of the Catholic Church," *Tavis Smiley, PBS,* February 22, 2013. Television.

Economic Justice

The level of poverty in the U.S. is astounding. With over 47 million people destitute and poverty having the greatest impact on Latino/as, African Americans, and women, oppressive structures clearly continue to serve their purpose. Jesus lived in a society in which many people suffered as a result of such power structures. Little has changed in the twenty-first century. We don't physically crucify people along our busy streets. Instead we crucify them with social policies and oppressive structures that make it impossible for them to achieve the so-called American Dream. The political call of the "Our Father" applies today, just as it did in the first century.

While politicians cut taxes for the top one percent of the population, the "other" 99 percent struggles to climb out of this economic mess dumped upon them. "Income inequality in the U.S. exceeds [that of] any other democracy in the developed world."[1] The wealth disparity continues to worsen and "is more extreme than anytime during the Great Depression."[2]

In addition, our cost of living is increasing at a much faster rate than the median household income. Likewise, the oppressive structures that exist in American culture keep more

---

1 Mortimer B. Zuckerman, "Making a Mockery of the American Dream," *U.S. News,* March 27, 2015. Retrieved from http://www.usnews.com/opinion/articles/2015/03/27/income-inequality-makes-a-mockery-of-the-american-dream.

2 Chris Matthews, "Wealth Inequality in America is Worse Than You Think," *Fortune Magazine,* October 31, 2014. Retrieved from http://fortune.com/2014/10/31/inequality-wealth-income-us/.

than 20 percent of African Americans and Latino/as living in poverty. Women continue to earn far less than their male counterparts and while we often cite the seventy-seven cents on the dollar statistic, in fact that number does not accurately represent the salaries of women of color or mothers. Women of color experience a much wider wage gap with earnings ranging only 54 to 64 percent of white male salaries.[3] In addition, the poverty rate for elderly women 75 and older is double that of men in the same age category.[4]

When examining motherhood and its effects on wage earnings, we see that with every child birthed a woman's salary decreases — a devastating factor in itself, but far more detrimental when we consider the impact on single mothers and poverty rates. In fact, motherhood is the greatest determining factor of poverty.

Single mothers have the greatest struggle, not because of anything inherent in single motherhood, but because of low wages and poor social policy. While more than 80 percent of single mothers work 30 hours per week or more, they are disproportionately more likely to be employed in low income positions. Discrimination against mothers in the workforce has led to decreased hiring rates and wages, lower-level positions, and fewer promotions.[5]

3 See Center for American Progress, "Women of Color and the Gender Wage Gap," April 14, 2015. Retrieved from https://www.americanprogress.org/issues/women/report/2015/04/14/110962/women-of-color-and-the-gender-wage-gap/.

4 See The U.S. Census Report "Income and Poverty in the United States: 2014" September 2015. Retrieved from: http://www.census.gov/content/dam/Census/library/publications/2015/demo/p60-252.pdf. Also see Gillian B. White, "America's Poverty Problem Hasn't Changed," *The Atlantic*, September 16, 2015. Retrieved from http://www.theatlantic.com/business/archive/2015/09/americas-poverty-problem/405700/.

5 Gina Messina-Dysert, "Why We Still Need a Feminist Agenda," *The*

While only about 6 percent of households headed by married couples live below the poverty line, over 30 percent of single mother households are impoverished. In addition, an astounding forty-five percent of children in single parent households live in poverty.[6]

Politicians have suggested various policies to combat the ongoing poverty issues in the U.S., yet none has been successful. You may remember now Speaker of the House Paul Ryan's proposed budget that called for drastic cuts to social programs for the poor — one that he claimed was informed by his Catholic identity and Catholic social teaching (CST). He was quickly criticized — and rightly so — by the U.S. Catholic Bishops, Catholic scholars, and perhaps most notably, the Nuns on the Bus. As Gerald Beyer pointed out, "he badly misunderstands two bedrock principles of CST — solidarity and subsidiarity. He also misinterprets how these principles apply to the scourge of poverty in the United States."[7]

Nuns on the Bus was formed by Sr. Simone Campbell, executive director of Network, a liberal social justice lobby in Washington, DC. She, along with eleven other nuns, toured the country on a bus, meeting with people to discuss the issues

Huffington Post, April 29, 2014. Retrieved from http://www.huffingtonpost.com/gina-messinadysert/why-we-still-need-a-femin_b_5232359.html.

6 See The U.S. Census Report "Income and Poverty in the United States: 2014," September 2015. Retrieved from http://www.census.gov/content/dam/Census/library/publications/2015/demo/p60-252.pdf. Also see Gillian B. White, "America's Poverty Problem Hasn't Changed," *The Atlantic*, September 16, 2015. Retrieved from http://www.theatlantic.com/business/archive/2015/09/americas-poverty-problem/405700/.

7 Gerald J. Beyer, "What Ryan Missed: What Catholic Social Teaching Says about Solidarity and Subsidiarity," *America Magazine*, June 4, 2012. Retrieved from http://americamagazine.org/issue/5143/100/what-ryan-missed.

with Ryan's budget and the necessity for policies that respond to the needs of the poor. There was an overwhelming response, and Nuns on the Bus was influential in shaping the conversation on policies, budget issues, and an appropriate response to the disenfranchised. If you haven't seen "#NunTrouble (It's All About that Bus),"[8] google it. You can thank me later.

So with whom would Jesus stand? Paul Ryan, who claims Catholic social teaching as his basis for cutting programs that aid the poor, or Sr. Simone Campbell and Nuns on the Bus, who continue to travel the country to call for social policy that assists the nation's most vulnerable persons? Looking at Jesus' teachings on standing with the oppressed and working against the larger establishments that functions to marginalize "the least of these," I think the answer is clear.

Occupy Wall Street

Fed up with Congress and the lack of action to support the needs of the people, Occupy Wall Street (OWS) was launched on September 17, 2011 in Manhattan's Financial District. Inspired by the uprisings in Egypt and Tunisia, OWS is a movement powered by the people that sought to "[fight] back against the corrosive power of major banks and multinational corporations over the democratic process, and the role of Wall Street in creating an economic collapse that has caused the greatest recession in generations."[9] The Internet group Anonymous

---

8 "#NunTrouble (It's All About that Bus)" is accessible at http://networklobby.org/bus2015.

9 "About," Occupy Wall Street. Retrieved from http://occupywallst.org/about/.

joined the #Occupy movement and called its followers to "flood lower Manhattan, set up tents, kitchens, peaceful barricades and occupy Wall Street," calling it "the financial Gommorah of America."[10] Followers launched action in over a hundred U.S. cities and fifteen hundred cities globally. People were inspired to reclaim power and demand accountability for big banks' corrupt practices that were making people destitute. Through social media platforms such as Twitter and Facebook, OWS reached a critical mass and continues to play a significant role in the global protest against the marginalization and impoverishment of millions.

A major supporter of OWS, Massachusetts Senator, Elizabeth Warren was the force behind the Obama consumer-protection bureau. She continues to challenge Wall Street and big banks for their excessive and predatory ways.[11] Republicans have attacked her for her avid support for the welfare of the people and she's been referred to as "a guileless, fevered Marxist."[12] Nonetheless, she has maintained her focus on protecting consumers from predatory banks and ending the "too big to fail" era. According to Warren, "if the regulators won't end 'too big to fail,' then Congress must act to protect our economy and prevent future crises."[13]

10 Adbusters, "Anonymous Joins #OCCUPYWALLSTREET," Adbusters Culturejammer Headquarters. *Adbusters.* August 23, 2011. Retrieved from https://www.adbusters.org/blogs/adbusters-blog/occupywallstreet.html.

11 See Elizabeth Warren, *A Fighting Chance* (New York: Metropolitan Books, 2014).

12 Jeffrey Lord, "Elizabeth Warren Becomes Obama's Albatross," *The American Spectator,* September 27, 2011. Retrieved from http://spectator.org/articles/36876/elizabeth-warren-becomes-obamas-albatross.

13 Warren quoted in Luke Johnson. "Elizabeth Warren: 'Too Big to Fail is Worse than Before Financial Crisis.' *The Huffington Post.* November 12, 2013.

Before Occupy Wall Street there was Occupy Temple. You may remember the incident described in the Gospels when Jesus threw his "temple tantrum" (Mark 11:15-19). What you may not realize is that this was not just an outburst of anger, but rather a planned attack to protest economic injustice. In addition, it was most likely the event that sealed Jesus' fate and led to his crucifixion. Jesus certainly realized that he was putting his life on the line with such a stunt. Nonetheless, he recognized such radical action as necessary to draw attention to the government's ongoing marginalization of the Jews.

"A den of robbers" is how Jesus referred to the Temple as he confronted the brokers who took advantage of every opportunity to bilk the pilgrims who traveled through Jerusalem for Passover. Conspiring with the priestly class, the brokers made the Temple a powerful economic center in Jerusalem. No different from the bankers today (in fact, "den of robbers" would be a very fair term to describe big banks), these "robbers" schemed to charge interest and fees to line their own pockets and plunge the Jewish people further in debt. Such practices violated Jewish tradition; collecting interest was prohibited, especially for those who were impoverished. Jesus was outraged by the betrayal and the predatory behavior "to the point where he physically disrupted the largest national bank in Israel during the height of its Passover practice of ripping off the poor and affluent pilgrims alike."[14]

Retrieved from http://www.huffingtonpost.com/2013/11/12/elizabeth-warren-too-big-to-fail_n_4260871.html.

14 Susan Brooks Thistlethwaite, *Occupy the Bible: What Jesus Really Said (and Did) About Money and Power*, (Eugene, Oregon: Wipf and Stock, 2012), xii.

Jesus occupied space as a method throughout his ministry beginning with Nazareth and on to Galilee, Jerusalem, and finally, Calvary. He did so by relating the places he occupied to Hebrew scripture and the teachings of the prophets. However, Jesus not only used occupation to take space, but also to "take possession." Susan Brooks Thistlethwaite explains this, saying "it also means to engage in struggle to live out of a different reality, to not let yourself be defined by others, but take back your own life, society, economy, and spiritual meaning from those who want to control you."[15] Through his preaching, Jesus called his followers to break away from the abuse and control of the Kingdom of Caesar and live out the Kingdom of God in the "here and now."

In addition to confronting the Roman Empire for its colonization of Israel, he also confronted the Temple elites for their problematic interpretations of Jewish texts.

> Jesus not only literally occupied the rural and urban areas of his time...he also took back the interpretation of the sacred texts from those who were using the scripture, in his time, to justify driving people into poverty through increased debt and low wages, and driving them out of their homes and jobs.[16]

If Jesus were alive today I imagine he would be in a tent somewhere with the #Occupy movement or perhaps riding on a bus full of nuns.

---

15 Ibid.
16 Ibid., xii-xiii.

If we look at Jesus' teachings, we can draw conclusions on how they could apply to our world today. And when it comes to economic injustice, there is no other issue Jesus spent more time discussing. Jesus believed that every person should have his or her fair share. He was opposed to materialism and called people to reject societal standards, leave their belongings to the poor, and focus on the important issues in life. Ending oppression was at the top of his list. In order to accomplish that, he knew economic justice must exist for all.

Occupy Temple is an important example of how Jesus would respond to the big banks and Wall Street, the ongoing oppression of the greater community, and the growing gap between the rich and poor. When we consider critical issues related to economic justice, we can learn where Jesus would stand based on the gospels.

Labor is a critical issue for Jesus. In fact, Crossan argues that Jesus created a union through his ministry. He points out that Jesus made a conscious effort to seek his followers in the Galilee rather than in his hometown of Nazareth. This is a critical observation. Jesus could have invited people to join his ministry from anywhere; why travel to the Galilee? The answer is simple. The fishing industry was being commercialized by the Roman Empire during this time. Because of this, the indigenous fishing industry was being regulated and heavily taxed to the point that profits were nil.[17]

17 See John Dominic Crossan, *God and Empire: Jesus Against Rome Then and Now* (New York: HarperOne, 2008). Crossan notes that the archeological discovery of sunken fishing boat in 1986 that surfaced during the drought that caused the Sea of Galilee to dwindle is evidence of the diminished fishing indus-

Jesus sought out those fishermen because he wanted to connect with people who had experienced imperial Rome's crushing power and the Kingdom of Caesar, which had forced them into poverty. Thistlethwaite explains,

> When Jesus went to the Sea of Galilee to start his ministry, he was not just calling individual disciples. He was starting a movement among those who would see the difference between the rule of the divine Caesar under the repression of the Roman occupiers and their Jewish collaborators, and what Jesus called the Kingdom of God.[18]

We can extrapolate from this that Jesus did in fact organize labor and that labor justice was an important part of his ministry. "Jesus organized workers into his disciples because they were the people who understood the difference between work as exploitation in the service of greed and work as a means to feed their families and benefit their communities."[19]

Jesus believed that the economy existed for the people, not the other way around. It is reasonable to conclude that the success of an economic institution would be based on how well it protects the dignity and life of every person. For Jesus, the quality of life for those who are most vulnerable is the measure of success of the economy. Do the people have access to shelter, food, clothing, education, healthcare, etc.? Do opportunities exist for work with just wages, safe environments, and bene-

---

try. The vessel dates to Jesus' time and the Roman occupation of Israel. What was found is a boat that was re-patched multiple times until it was so worn it had no more use. Had the industry continue to be profitable, a boat in such poor condition would have never been used.

18 Thistlethwaite, 39.
19 Ibid., 40.

fits? Jesus is clear that we are all moral agents when it comes to economic life. Through our daily purchasing and investment decisions, we participate in shaping our economy; and thus, we must each recognize our economic choices as political statements. However, we must also understand that governmental action is necessary to support society's moral obligation to provide for individual needs, protect human rights, and pursue economic justice.

Healthcare

The Affordable Care Act (ACA) — or Obamacare — is a central issue for Trump and the GOP. Republicans vow to repeal the Act, arguing that healthcare should be privatized, and Democrats argue that a government-run system is necessary to ensure every person has access to healthcare.

The issue of healthcare easily falls into the category of economic justice. If the people's needs are holy, then healthcare is a right, not a privilege. It is the disenfranchised who lack access to healthcare and their wellbeing suffers as a result. And from what has been discussed thus far, there is no doubt that Jesus' main concern was for the poor, the oppressed, and those whom society had cast out.

Jesus was a healer. As a compassionate prophet he reached out to those in need and sought to heal those with the greatest afflictions. Would Jesus support government run healthcare? Or would he claim that the nation should empower individuals and families to make their own decisions about healthcare? Or even perhaps that we should trust in God alone to meet our needs?

When the ACA was passed, megachurch pastor, Rick Warren — who also delivered the invocation at Barack Obama's inauguration — tweeted that he would rather go to jail than give into Obamacare.[1] Many Christians, like Warren, think Je-

1 Rick Warren's tweet read "I'd go to jail rather than cave in to a government mandate that violates what God commands us to do. Would you? Acts 5:29."

sus would stand against Obamacare for a number of reasons. To begin with, some fear that it will fund abortion and birth control[2] although the mandate includes an exemption for churches. Some argue that the quality of care will be diminished, particularly for terminal patients. Others claim that Jesus would never support any political solution. According to Carl Raschke, "Writing checks won't solve problems…One has to get involved. If we see someone in need, we just don't throw a dollar at him or her. You get to know them, you offer yourself and ask what you can do for them."[3] An argument with which Jesus would likely agree. Yet it is more complicated than this.

Some GOP lawmakers have used Christian scripture to justify the repeal of ACA. According to Republican Rep. Roger Marshall of Kansas, "Just like Jesus said, 'The poor will always be with us.' There is a group of people that just don't want health care and aren't going to take care of themselves."[4] Marshall must have overlooked the parts of the gospel stories where Jesus said to give all your belongings to the poor, and the part when he healed the poor, and the rest of the Gospels.

There are also many Christians who claim that Jesus

Retrieved from http://www.nationalreview.com/corner/290654/rick-warren-vs-hhs-mandate-rather-go-jail-cave-kathryn-jean-lopez.

2 Note that the issue of reproductive justice will be discussed in detail later in this chapter.

3 Carl Raschke quoted in John Blake, "Would Jesus Support Health Care Reform?" *CNN Belief Blog*, June 28, 2012. Retrieved from http://religion.blogs.cnn.com/2012/06/28/would-jesus-support-healthcare-reform/comment-page-11/.

4 Roger Marshall quoted in Jack Jenkins, "The Strange Origins of the GOP Ideology that Rejects Caring for the Poor," *Think Progress,* June 9, 2017. Retrieved from https://thinkprogress.org/bad-theology-conservative-benefits-1d42ef90b387.

would support Obamacare. Jesus argued that the health of a society could be measured by how well it cares for its poor. According to John Kraftchick, "A move toward universal health-care would be fitting with the prophetic tradition."[5] Likewise, Christian Piatt states,

> As a Christian, I think it's a matter of justice. To suggest that my personal right to have more choices supersedes the right of every person to have access to even basic healthcare is an un-Christ-like attitude. And although there certainly are other means of achieving this (single payer being one), no one else has dared to push a serious agenda of reform until now.[6]

Interestingly, Republican Ohio Governor John Kasich, although not a supporter of Obamacare, does support elements relating to expansion of Medicaid, and does so citing his religious beliefs. He stated, "When you die and get to the meeting with St. Peter, he's probably not going to ask you much about what you did about keeping government small, but he's going to ask you what you did for the poor. You'd better have a good answer."[7]

---

5 John Kraftchick quoted in John Blake, "Would Jesus Support Health Care Reform?" *CNN Belief Blog*, June 28, 2012. Retrieved from http://religion.blogs.cnn.com/2012/06/28/would-jesus-support-healthcare-reform/comment-page-11/.

6 Christian Piatt, "Health Care is a Moral and Religious Issue," *Sojourners*, October 30, 2013. Retrieved from https://sojo.net/articles/health-care-moral-and-religious-issue?utm_source=feedburner&utm_medium=feed&utm_campaign=Feed%253A%20sojourners%252Fblog%20%28Sojourners%20Blog%20Feed%29.

7 John Kasich quoted in Brendan Bordelon, "Is John Kasich's Presidential Run for Real?" *The National Review*, April 23, 2015. Retrieved from http://www.nationalreview.com/article/417388/john-kasichs-presidential-run-real-brendan-bordelon.

While both sides agree that Jesus would focus on aiding the disenfranchised, they disagree on how he would get there. Jesus was anti-establishment. But does that mean he would be opposed to government healthcare? Under the Roman Empire, surely no such thing existed. But if the intentions of the leader, of the nation, are good, would Jesus approve of a government program?

Democrats and Republicans argue about the size of government and debates on social policy stem from there. However, may I suggest that perhaps government size is the wrong question on which to focus? Perhaps instead we should focus on the quality and purpose of government — compassion and care for the common good of all people. Wouldn't healthcare fit into that model?

If we turn to the Gospels and consider Jesus' teachings, the answer is not as muddied as some think. In Matthew 25: 31-46 we find the parable of the Judgment of the Nations. The parable compares two nations, one that cares for the needs of the people, and one that does not. "Truly I tell you, just as you did not do it to one of the least of these, you did not do it to me.' And these will go away into eternal punishment, but the righteous into eternal life" (Matthew 25:45-6). Jesus acknowledges the possibility of a nation with the common good of the people at its center. And so, if such a model could be established, then Jesus' teachings would support government healthcare.

Obamacare may not have been the right answer; but

its passing had a positive intent. Perhaps, we should consider Obamacare a step in the right direction; a move toward a healthcare system that provides for the medical needs of every person regardless of wealth. Revision is a part of life. Almost nothing comes together perfectly on the first try — just ask Steve Jobs.

As I write this, the U.S. is awaiting a vote on Trumpcare, a plan that Trump himself has called "mean." The bill is being drafted by a handful of Republicans in secret and what it proposes is anyone's guess. Democrats have called the level of secrecy "shameful" and "absurd." The tables were turned in 2009-10 when the Affordable Care Act was up for vote. Now Vice President Mike Pence criticized the bill with the same complaint: that something that will affect everyone in the nation should not be determined behind closed doors. Nonetheless, the processes of Trumpcare and Obamacare have notable differences. While Trumpcare has been developed in total secrecy, the ACA was debated for twenty-five days on the floor and was reviewed in numerous public bipartisan hearings.[8]

The bottom line is that the healthcare of millions of Americans is at stake, and the GOP is focused on pushing through a bill to fulfill the promise of repealing the ACA while giving no serious consideration to what a revision would look like. With well-intentioned effort and a focus on the people rather than government size or party politics, a just healthcare system implemented by the nation is possible. However, under

---

8 Emma Talkoff, "Mike Pence's Obamacare Tweet Came Back to Haunt Him," *Time Magazine,* June 20, 2017.

the Trump Administration there is little hope that this can happen.

Education

Education is likely the most ambitious and challenging project for our nation. It seeks to develop smart, caring, and ethical human beings who will become the next generation of leaders in our country. Beyond this enormous task, it seeks to do so in a consistent manner for all children. However, all children do not learn the same way, and many are disadvantaged before they are even born.

While we tout the American Dream — that anyone can achieve her or his goals through hard work and education — studies demonstrate that this is simply not true. Economic injustice has a critical impact on education and success. Likewise, social mobility is dwindling, and those born poor generally stay poor.[1] According to the National Center for Education Statistics, more than fifty percent of students across the U.S. are living in poverty, a number that continues to grow.

Opportunities for children from middle-class or privileged backgrounds are more available than for children born into poverty. In fact, a well-known study completed by the University of Kansas demonstrates that by age three, children in low-income households hear thirty million fewer words than children who are living in homes with higher economic levels.[2]

1 Howard Steven Friedman, "The American Myth of Social Mobility," *The Huffington Post*, September 15, 2012. Retrieved from http://www.huffingtonpost.com/howard-steven-friedman/class-mobility_b_1676931.html.

2 Betty Hart and Todd Risley, *Meaningful Differences in Everyday Experience of Young American Children* (Baltimore, MD: Brookes Publishing, 1995); Betty Hart and Todd Risley, "The early catastrophe: The 30 million word gap by age

In addition, children in middle-class homes or above are exposed to higher quality conversations.[3]

Beyond the differences in words and conversations to which children are exposed, other external factors also play a critical role in their learning. Fetuses that are exposed to drugs, stress, violence, environmental toxins and poor nutrition in utero have cognitive development issues that can begin in the prenatal stages and last through adulthood. Such factors are far more prevalent in low-income households. Likewise, children who are raised in poverty often have low self-esteem, difficulty making decisions and planning ahead, poor impulse control, and struggle with managing emotions.

The high level of inequality that exists means that standardized testing or a single approach to improving education is not useful. Likewise, early childhood education is an equity issue. Families who live below the poverty wage cannot afford additional tuition to give their children the head start needed to prepare for kindergarten. Hence, children begin their K-12 school careers at different developmental stages and with different abilities.

The newly appointed Secretary of Education and major Republican donor, Betsy Devos, brings many issues to her new position. Her nomination for the position was odd given her lack of experience and knowledge in education. Because of

---

3." *American Educator,* (2003), 27(1): 4 – 9.

　　3 Anne Fernald and Adriana Weisleder, "Twenty years after Meaningful Differences, it's time to reframe the 'deficit' debate about the importance of children's early language experience," *Human Development,* (2015), 58(x): 1 – 4.

her own privileged background, she has never had to deal with financial aid; all of her children attended elite schools and completed college with no student loans. When questioned during her confirmation hearing, she performed very poorly and was unable to answer basic questions. Notably, when Senator Al Franken asked what her views are on proficiency versus growth (earning a score that is deemed proficient versus measuring student improvement), she was unable to respond because she was unfamiliar with the debate. When asked whether she thought there was a place for guns in schools, Devos responded yes, citing possible grizzly bear attacks. Her nomination was highly contested and for the first time in American history, the Vice President had to cast the deciding vote to confirm a candidate.

Devos has developed an education plan that is in direct conflict with Christian values. Three major policies Devos supports have reinforced the marginalization of children living in poverty, children of color, and children with special needs. To begin with, she is a proponent of privatizing education. This is highly problematic given that such a structure serves those who are privileged. It also drives public funding away from public schools and instead goes to charter schools and other specialized programs. While Devos claims that privatizing education would offer better support to Christian schools and allow for individual freedom, in reality it will create an unjust distribution of resources that benefit the wealthy and further disadvantage the marginalized.

Arguing that certain protections should be regulated at

the state level, Devos has also indicated that free education for children with special needs will no longer be guaranteed by federal regulations. Such action will create disparity and resources needed will be unavailable to those in the greatest need. Without federal regulations to hold schools accountable, the most vulnerable children in our nation will suffer.[4]

Devos has lived a life of incredible privilege, one that creates a disconnect with those who are in the greatest need of a good education provided through the public school system. She lacks awareness of systematic oppression and because of that is focused on "school choice," which only benefits those who have financial resources. As Secretary of Education, she has a moral obligation to enact programs that will educate and protect all children.

Education reform should focus on reducing the impact of poverty on educational achievement. And this would require that as a nation we give far more attention to the economic disparities overall. Given his focus on ending poverty, Jesus would recognize that the education gap is directly linked to economic injustice and that the current administration has no interest in assisting those who are disenfranchised.

---

4 See Rachel Lam, "How Betsy Devos' Education Plan is at Odds with Christian Values," *Sojourners,* May 2017. Retrieved from https://sojo.net/magazine/may-2017/devos-plan-education-against-Christian-values.

Immigration

Immigration has become a discriminatory issue in this nation. With fear, xenophobia, and greed at the fore front, we have become desensitized to the experience of those coming to the U.S. Most of us can only imagine what it must be like to leave behind one's home; a safe haven that in some instances has become a threat. Leaving behind one's family, culture, and those comforts that we only associate with home is surely detrimental. Often times, making it across the border means a very different life than a person has led in her or his homeland. Violence has disrupted any opportunity to return home and you are deemed the "other" in a new country that presents different but equally damaging forms of brutality.

We are misguided when it comes to particular issues related to immigration. Many people argue that undocumented immigrants do not pay taxes, are a drain on our economy, cause crime rates to increase, and take jobs away from Americans. In fact, every person pays taxes with each purchase he or she makes, as well as property tax regardless of whether one owns or rents a home. Likewise, statistics show that nearly three quarters of undocumented immigrants pay both state and federal taxes.[1] Beyond these factors, The American Farm Bureau

---

1 See Justice for Immigrants, "Countering the Myths," Retrieved from http://www.justiceforimmigrants.org/myths.shtml. Also see Immigration Policy Center, "Undocumented Immigrants as Taxpayers," (November 2007) Retrieved from http://www.americanimmigrationcouncil.org/sites/default/files/docs/Undocumented%20as%20Taxpayer%2011-29-07_0.pdf; Eduardo Porter, "Illegal Immigrants are Bolstering Social Security with Billions," *New York Times,* (April 5, 2005), Retrieved from: http://www.nytimes.com/2005/04/05/business/05im-

states that the U.S. economy would lose up to $9 billion a year in agricultural production if we did not welcome guest workers. Immigrants also boost the U.S. economy. Research by the CATO Institute and the President's Council of Economic Advisors demonstrates that immigrants pay $80,000 more in taxes than they collect in government services and for those with college degrees the fiscal return is $198,000.[2]

When it comes to American jobs, immigrants are playing a critical role in offsetting the decline of U.S.-born low wage earners. Research shows that undocumented immigrants commit fewer crimes than native born Americans. According to Harvard sociologist Robert Sampson, "first generation immigrants are 45 percent less likely to commit violent crimes than Americanized, third generation immigrants."[3]

Although our nation was founded on the backs of immigrants, policy proposals today are becoming more and more hardline. Security concerns, socioeconomic factors, and cultural factions stand at the center of debates. Even language has become a dividing factor among the right and left. Democrats use the term "undocumented" to describe the status of a per-

migration.html?ex=1270353600&en=78c87ac4641dc383&ei=5090&partner=kmarx - See more at http://www.justiceforimmigrants.org/myths.shtml#sthash.d4u2uoMF.dpuf.

2 Justice for Immigrants, "Countering the Myths," Retrieved from http://www.justiceforimmigrants.org/myths.shtml.

3 See Justice for Immigrants; Robert Sampson. "Open Doors Don't Invite Criminals," *The New York Times,* March 11, 2006, Retrieved from http://www.nytimes.com/2006/03/11/opinion/11sampson.html?_r=0; Executive Office of the President: Council of Economic Advisors, "Immigration's Economic Impact," June 20, 2007. Retrieved from http://www.whitehouse.gov/cea/cea_immigration_062007.html.

son who entered the U.S. without proper documentation while maintaining a focus on one's humanity. Republicans use the term "illegal" as a way to denote that one has broken the law. And yet we do not refer to any other criminal as an "illegal." So, one must question whether this is an appropriate term in the case of immigration, or whether it is being used as a way to further degrade a person who has been deemed the "other." I wonder how we would refer to Jesus — as undocumented or illegal? After all, he was a refugee. And which of these terms would Jesus use? I cannot imagine that "illegal" would fit in with Jesus' ideology.

Despite the fact that Trump did not invent the conversation on immigration as he has suggested, his argument that the U.S. should deport approximately 12 million immigrants is shaping the Republican debate on this issue. Calling for a great wall and harsher laws to keep the "other" out, Trump argues that the leaders of Mexico have taken advantage of the U.S. "by using illegal immigration to export the crime and poverty in their own country."[4] While Republicans have harshly criticized Trump's notion that deporting 12 million immigrants is a realistic plan, many of their proposals are similar in that they call for stronger borders, deportation in some or all cases, and a rigorous path to citizenship - one that most U.S. citizens would not be able to complete.

The Democratic approach to the issue of immigration likewise calls for border control; however, there is a stronger

4 Donald Trump, "Immigration Reform that Will Make America Great Again," Positions. Retrieved from https://www.donaldjtrump.com/positions/immigration-reform.

focus on the benefits of immigration for the U.S. Rather than arguing that undocumented immigrants are stealing American jobs, Democrats generally discuss immigration as a way to build our economy, support families, and strengthen our nation. Likewise, Democrats see deportation programs and detention centers as a violation of human rights and predominantly seek to address immigrants who are in the U.S. illegally in a way that acknowledges the dignity of the individual.

While I do appreciate the sentiment of wanting to protect our nation's borders and focus on security, such a system ignores the many who seek passage into the U.S. as a means of escaping severe economic and physical violence. What about those who need safe refuge? What about those who seek the American Dream for themselves and their families? Democratic policies, although not perfect, are much more in line with the teachings of Jesus and the idea that we should always extend ourselves to those who need help. Although some people argue that this is not a responsibility of the U.S., if we are basing our ideas and our votes on the teachings of Jesus, we need to rethink either our positions or our faith.

Although we think of immigration predominantly in terms of the American-Mexican border - a matter of bigotry, really - the issue has become much more complex in an age of terrorism and fear mongering. With recent terror attacks across the globe including here in the U.S., Trump has called for a ban on Muslims — again playing on the fears of the public and encouraging hate speech and violence. Yet both Democrats and Republicans have harshly criticized Trump's outlandish statements, noting that such a ban is unconstitutional. Likewise, both sides agree that Trump's speech encourages hate in our nation and offers justification to ISIS for their targeted attacks.

As the Syrian refugee crisis intensified, Republicans demanded that the U.S. close its borders and refuse entry in fear that a terrorist may gain passage by posing as a refugee. Speaker of the House Paul Ryan called for a moratorium on Syrian refugees entering the U.S. claiming that many want to take advantage of the nation's compassion. The House of Representatives followed up by voting overwhelmingly to change the vetting process for Syrians, urging that we subject them to the highest level of security checks for any traveler to the U.S. It seems that the Republicans, and Trump specifically, have launched the New Red Scare.[5] Sadly, many Americans are buying into his idea hook, line, and sinker.

While I do not want to discount efforts to create a safe environment for American citizens, it is also necessary to point out that the likelihood of a terrorist making his or her way into the States as a refugee are slim. In addition, the terrorist attacks that the U.S. has endured were not a result of any refugee entering the nation. And finally, to accuse all Muslims of being terrorists is like accusing all Christians of being abortion clinic bombers. It doesn't make sense. Extremism is a serious issue, but we should not view it differently from one tradition or culture to another. The issue is that we fear what we don't know

5 The Red Scare refers to the hysteria that existed in the U.S. during late 1940's and early 1950's when the Cold War between the Soviet Union and the U.S. intensified due to the perception that Communism posed a threat to the nation.

— and this is another reason why we have worked so hard to create a Jesus that is a reflection of ourselves.

If we look to the Gospels, teachings on immigration and support for refugees are clear. First, Jesus was a refugee. Not too long ago, someone posted on my Facebook page that Jesus was not a refugee, that he had a home, and was only born in a manger because Mary and Joseph were traveling. "So stop calling him a refugee!"

While the innkeepers provided safe haven for Mary, Joseph, and the birth of Jesus in the Gospel of Luke, this commenter had forgotten that the Holy Family fled to Egypt to protect Jesus' life when Herod had all boys ages two and under slaughtered. Yes, Jesus was a refugee (Matthew 2:13-15). And we should not forget Jesus' words: "I was a stranger, and you invited me in" (Matthew 25:35).

Jesus' teachings throughout the Gospels are easily related to the issue of immigration. Beyond his teaching in Matthew, Jesus calls us to "Bring good news to the poor...release to the captives...sight to the blind...and let the oppressed go free" (Luke 4:16-21). He states, "Whoever has two coats must share with anyone who has none; and whoever has food must do likewise" (Luke 3:11).

Even beyond the Gospels, immigration is an ongoing theme in the Bible. In Romans, Paul states that the mark of the true Christian is one who "extend(s) hospitality to strangers" (12:13). In II Corinthians 8:13-15 we read, "It is a question of a

fair balance between your present abundance and their need."
And in Ephesians 2: 11-22, "So then you are no longer strangers
and aliens, but you are citizens with the saints and also members of the household of God."

Our biblical patriarchs and matriarchs were refugees
and God passes judgment based on how one responds to the
stranger. Many of us are familiar with the story of Sodom and
Gomorrah (Genesis 19),[6] but are confused about the true meaning of the text. This is one of the five texts in the Bible that are
claimed as support for the oppression of the LGBTQIA community. However, Sodom and Gomorrah is actually about hospitality, about welcoming the stranger, and it highlights issues
related to the immigration debate.

If we examine the story closely and in its full context, we
learn that Lot is spared because he welcomed the strangers into
his home, fed them, cared for them, and protected them from
the townsmen. God shows mercy to Lot because he honored
God's call to be hospitable to the stranger. We are all called to
recognize the stranger in need and offer hospitality; this directly relates to the immigrants and refugees seeking a safe haven
in the U.S.

Referring to the status of Jesus as an immigrant, his
own teachings, and the biblical text overall, it is clear that Jesus
stands on the side of the disenfranchised. In our society, there
are few persons more persecuted than immigrants. How Jesus
would address the issue of immigration is another question.

---

6 The section on "Marriage Equality" focuses in greater detail on Genesis 19.

But it is more than reasonable to say that Jesus would not agree with proposals that call for deportation, detention, family separation, or any other form of injustice against immigrants — a population already suffering and in great need.

And so, for the politicians who use the Christian faith as a means to get elected, yet fail to observe the biblical mandate proclaimed by a refugee... Lord, in your mercy, hear our prayers.

Gun Control

Particularly throughout the midwest and the south, many people associate their right to own a gun with their Christian religious values. I personally find this confusing given Jesus' stance on non-violence.

Gun control versus gun rights is a complicated issue stemming from the Second Amendment: "A well regulated militia being necessary to the security of a free state, the right of the people to keep and bear arms shall not be infringed." The debate centers on whether the Constitution is giving the right to own a gun to every individual, or only to those citizens who make up the body of the military. Those who want gun control argue that bearing arms is a collective right, whereas advocates of gun rights claim that gun ownership is necessary for protection and self-defense.

The gap in the gun control debate has grown substantially in the last few decades. During his presidency, Ronald Reagan argued, "I do not believe in taking away the right of the citizen for sporting, for hunting and so forth, or for home defense. But I do believe that an AK-47, a machine gun, is not a sporting weapon or needed for defense of a home."[1] I don't disagree with this position, and neither do most people who seek gun control. However, the debate has become about party lines rather than a reasonable law that honors rights while being

---

1 Ronald Reagan, University of Southern California, Los Angeles, CA, February 6, 1989.

committed to safety.

In 2015 there were more mass shootings in the U.S. than days in the year. In fact, the U.S. has one of the highest murder rates of developing countries with nearly three quarters of those murders being committed with a gun. In addition, gun control is a serious women's issue given that most women victims who are killed by a gun are murdered by someone they know. Following the mass shooting at Umpqua Community College on October 1, 2015, Obama commented, "Tally up the number of Americans who've been killed through terrorist attacks over the last decade and the number of Americans who've been killed by gun violence, and post those side-by-side."[2] So here are those numbers:

From 2005-2015[3]

- *Americans killed in terror attacks on U.S. soil: 71*
- *Americans killed by gun violence in the U.S.: 301,797*

Whether you are an Obama supporter or not, you have to admit, the numbers don't lie. Nonetheless, mass shootings only account for about 2 percent of gun deaths annually. Most of those killed by guns are murdered in situations ranging from

---

2 Barack Obama quoted in Erik Wemple, "President Obama, National Assignment Editor," *The Washington Post,* October 2, 2015. Retrieved from https://www.washingtonpost.com/blogs/erik-wemple/wp/2015/10/02/president-obama-national-assignment-editor/?utm_term=.9b34d3729360.

3 See Linda Qiu. "Fact-Checking a Comparison of Gun Deaths and Terrorism Deaths." *Politifact.* October 5, 2015. Retrieved from http://www.politifact.com/truth-o-meter/statements/2015/oct/05/viral-image/fact-checking-comparison-gun-deaths-and-terrorism-/.

domestic violence to arguments at the bar and to road rage; there are numerous situations that result in someone being murdered with a gun in the U.S. each year. When I hear Trump propose that there should be no such thing as a gun free zone, I wonder whether he is really looking at the issue with a critical eye. Then again, critical thinking does not seem to be Trump's strong suit.

Many Republicans don't disagree that some level of gun control needs to be passed. For instance, in January, 2013 now Speaker of the House, Paul Ryan stated: "I think we need to find out how to close these loopholes and do it in such a way that we don't infringe upon people's Second Amendment rights." He continued, "We had this issue, 2001, 1999 I think … when I first got into Congress. At the time I remember thinking, 'You know, there is a loophole here. We should address that.'"[4]

However, in January of 2016 when President Obama announced his executive action aimed at reducing gun violence, Ryan criticized him for being "dismissive" and called his actions unconstitutional. Focused on expanding background checks, registration for licensed gun dealers, and narrowing the gun show loophole, Obama's executive action mirrored Ryan's call for change in 2013. However, when the plan was proposed by a Democrat, Ryan argued,

We all are pained by the recent atrocities in our country, but no change the president is reportedly considering would

4 Paul Ryan quoted in Jennifer Bendery, "Paul Ryan Wants Someone to Close the Gun Show Loophole, as Long as that Somebody isn't Obama," *The Huffington Post,* January 4, 2016. Retrieved from http://www.huffingtonpost.com/entry/paul-ryan-gun-background-checks_568aec6ee4b0b958f65c9135.

have prevented them…At a time when the country wants the president to lead the fight against radical Islamic terror, this is yet another attempt to divide and distract from his failed policies.[5]

Likewise, Marco Rubio took to the airwaves claiming that Obama wanted to take away everyone's guns. While making that argument in an interview on Good Morning America, George Stephanopoulos called Rubio on the carpet. Barely backing down, Rubio acknowledged that the executive action actually would not take away gun owner rights, but continued that he strongly believed this to be Obama's ultimate goal. Rubio then followed up calling all citizens to purchase guns. On *Face the Nation* with John Dickerson, Rubio argued, "If ISIS were to visit us, or our communities, at any moment, the last line of defense between ISIS and my family is the ability that I have to protect my family from them, or from a criminal, or anyone else who seeks to do us harm. Millions of Americans feel that way."[6] Fear mongering rather than facts continues to play a critical role in our gun control debate.

While our politicians are obsessed with battling party lines and maintaining partisan stances, our "Christian" nation continues to be one of the most violent. If we fought so vigorously for every person's right to have food, clean water, and health care as we do for guns, where would we be as a nation? As a people? A global community? It seems that our politicians

5 Paul Ryan, "Statement on Potential Executive Action to Restrict 2nd Amendment Rights," Press Release, January 4, 2016. Retrieved from http://www.speaker.gov/press-release/speaker-ryan-potential-executive-action-restrict-2nd-amendment-rights.

6 Marco Rubio Interview, *Face the Nation*, CBS, January 17, 2016. Television.

are focused on personal vendettas rather than on putting the needs of the people first.

Although many persons would argue that gun ownership is a need of the people, Jesus would beg to differ. Guns did not exist in Jesus' time, yet there is much that can be interpreted from Jesus' teachings on this issue. Luke 22: 47-53 is the story of Jesus' arrest in which an apostle strikes a slave of the high priest with his sword cutting off his ear. Jesus responds by saying, "No more of this!…Put your sword back into its place; for all who take the sword will perish by the sword," and then heals the man's ear. As Jesus is being taken into custody to be crucified, he surely knows he will suffer and die. But his response is one of non-violence.

Non-violence and pacifism are key teachings of Jesus. In Matthew 5:38-41 Jesus discusses retaliation stating,

> You have heard that it was said, 'An eye for an eye and a tooth for a tooth.' But I say to you, Do not resist an evildoer. But if anyone strikes you on the right cheek, turn the other also; and if anyone wants to sue you and take your coat, give your cloak as well; and if anyone forces you to go one mile, go also the second mile.

Jesus calls us to love our enemies as ourselves. In Matthew 5:43-48 he states, "You have heard that it was said, 'You shall love your neighbor and hate your enemy.' But I say to you, Love your enemies and pray for those who persecute you, so that you may be children of your Father in heaven…[I]f you greet only your brothers and sisters, what more are you doing than others?"

If Jesus believed that we must lay our lives down before lifting the sword, then what need would a person have for a gun? Gun control is a complicated issue in the twenty-first century, and it would be unfair for me to claim that Jesus would support a particular policy on gun control. Nonetheless, if Jesus did not condone the sword to save his own life, I suspect he would not approve of Rubio's purchasing of a gun on Christmas Eve to protect his family from ISIS.

Marriage Equality

Just after the Supreme Court ruling that made same sex marriage legal across the U.S., many of us were captivated by Kim Davis proclaiming that "under the authority of God" she was refusing to issue marriage licenses to same sex couples. Nonetheless, her willingness to go to jail rather than abide by the law has made Davis a martyr of sorts. Mike Huckabee and Ted Cruz held a rally for Davis and celebrate her release from jail. Even Pope Francis met with Davis during his visit to the U.S., although many claim the pope was duped into the meeting. While the Vatican issued a statement confirming the meeting, later it issued a second statement - something that rarely happens. But in this situation, the pope wanted to make clear that the visit was not confirmation of support for Davis' position. Nonetheless, his statement to her, to "stay strong," left some confused about Francis' intent.

Although many see Pope Francis as liberal when it comes to social policy, and it is very likely that he was indeed duped into meeting with Davis, as I shared with Steve Kornacki about the Davis debacle,[1] our new rock star pope is a traditionalist when it comes to family. I appreciate that Pope Francis is taking steps toward reforming the Catholic Church. However he has also been clear that he supports a theology of complementarity and the idea that marriage is only between a man and

---

1 "Pope Francis confirms meeting with Kim Davis," *Today with Steve Kornacki, MSNBC*, September 30, 2015.

a woman.

Though her attorney has compared Davis to Martin Luther King, Jr., I am not so sure Jesus would agree. While King relied on Christian teachings to work toward uprooting oppression and achieving civil rights for African Americans, Davis has claimed a particular interpretation of a text and has used it to deny the rights of others. Though we are a secular nation and though legalizing marriage equality is based on federal law, not religion, Davis' claim of being a conscientious objector is without basis. No one was forcing Davis to do anything; she could have quit her job or asked to be assigned to a different role. Nonetheless, Davis proclaimed it God's will that she step in and deny the legal rights of individuals based on her own ideas about divinely ordained marriage. Without attacking Davis' character, one must question her ideas (and the ideas of many others like her) about the sanctity of heterosexual marriage when divorce rates are close to 50 percent and Davis herself has been married four times. And let's not forget the history of why marriage became the foundation of society — so that men could track their bloodlines, women's sexuality could be controlled, and gender roles could be reinforced.[2]

Such arguments — like Davis'— are based on the idea that the Bible condemns homosexuality. It is disappointing that many people prooftext the Bible — selecting one or two lines to focus on rather than reading them in context. Nonetheless, we are living in a time where it seems that critical thinking is

2 See Margaret A. Farley, *Just Love: A Framework for Christian Sexual Ethics*, (New York: Continuum, 2006) for an analysis of an historical overview of sexuality and marriage.

no longer the focus of our education system, and opinions are often formed on bits and pieces of information rather than examining all the facts.

To begin with, there are 31,102 verses in the Bible; of those, four are claimed to discuss homosexuality. Three are located in the Hebrew Bible and one is located in the New Testament, but none in the Gospels. Jesus never speaks on homosexuality, although he does discuss divorce and adultery. Perhaps someone should tell Kim Davis.

Over two thousand verses discuss money and economic justice, and those that focus on liberation and love are far too many to count. The Bible has an overarching theme of liberation, meaning that if you read the Bible and examine its texts from cover to cover, the overriding lesson we should take away is that human dignity should be honored and no person should be oppressed. Nonetheless, homosexuality is the one issue that some people cling to and make one of the hot button issues in the U.S. today.

The story of Sodom and Gomorrah (Genesis 19) is the first of the verses on which the homosexuality debate focuses.

> The two angels came to Sodom in the evening, and Lot was sitting in the gateway of Sodom. When Lot saw them, he rose to meet them, and bowed down with his face to the ground. He said, "Please, my lords, turn aside to your servant's house and spend the night, and wash your feet; then you can rise early and go on your way." They said, "No; we will spend the night in the square."

But he urged them strongly; so they turned aside to him and entered his house; and he made them a feast, and baked unleavened bread, and they ate. But before they lay down, the men of the city, the men of Sodom, both young and old, all the people to the last man, surrounded the house; and they called to Lot, "Where are the men who came to you tonight? Bring them out to us, so that we may know them." Lot went out of the door to the men, shut the door after him, and said, "I beg you, my brothers, do not act so wickedly. Look, I have two daughters who have not known a man; let me bring them out to you, and do to them as you please; only do nothing to these men, for they have come under the shelter of my roof." But they replied, "Stand back!" And they said, "This fellow came here as an alien, and he would play the judge! Now we will deal worse with you than with them." Then they pressed hard against the man Lot, and came near the door to break it down. But the men inside reached out their hands and brought Lot into the house with them, and shut the door. And they struck with blindness the men who were at the door of the house, both small and great, so that they were unable to find the door (Genesis 19: 1-11).

Later, Lot and his family are told by the angels to leave the city and not look back. The town is obliterated.

We've become obsessed with this text as confirmation that homosexuality should be condemned; why else would God destroy the land? Interestingly, we generally focus on the men of Sodom wanting to rape or "know" the angels. Yet, we ignore other key parts of the text: Lot welcomes the angels and Lot's willingness to give up his virgin daughters to be gang raped.

It is abhorrent but no surprise that we ignore the threat against Lot's daughters; violence against women continues to be of little consequence today. But more on that later.

Sodom and Gomorrah presents the story of Lot, a man who welcomed the stranger and protected them from violence that was threatened because they were not citizens of Sodom. As I stated earlier, this text is not about homosexuality; it is about the treatment of the foreigner and the poor.[3] This Ezekiel 16:49 states clearly; the text is ignored although it explicitly relates to the story of Sodom and Gomorrah: "This was the guilt of your sister Sodom: she and her daughters had pride, excess of food, and prosperous ease, but did not aid the poor and needy." We might consider how this verse relates to the U.S. today, especially under a Trump Administration.

Two texts are presented in Leviticus, a book that is focused on laws:

- "You shall not lie with a male as with a woman; it is an abomination," (18:22); and

- "If a man lies with a male as with a woman, both of them have committed an abomination; they shall be put to death; their blood is upon them," (20:13).

Okay, this may seem pretty clear cut; but if you read these verses in context rather than prooftexting, you come to

---

3 See Jay Johnson, "The Bible and Same-Sex Relationships: Fictions and Facts," Resources, The Center for Lesbian and Gay Studies in Religion and Ministry. August 31, 2011. Retrieved from http://clgs.org/multimedia-archive/the-bible-and-same-sex-relationships-fictions-and-facts/.

find that they are a part of many laws we would never implement today. Dr. Laura, the well-known radio host, made the
mistake of sharing her opinion on homosexuality on her show
referencing the book of Leviticus. A letter from a listener soon
followed pointing out that she had picked out a sentence from
the scripture and ignored the rest of the content. What Dr. Laura did not note is that the law books of the Torah also state that
you:

- can sell your daughter into slavery (Exodus 21:7),

- can own slaves from neighboring nations (Leviticus 25:44),

- cannot have contact with women while they are menstru-
  ating (Leviticus 15:19-24),

- can execute anyone who works on the Sabbath (Exodus 35:2),

- cannot eat shellfish because it is an abomination (Leviticus 11:10),

- cannot approach the altar of God if you have poor eye-
  sight (Leviticus 21:20),

- cannot plant two different crops in the same field (Leviticus 19:19).[4]

The point here is that we no longer follow these other rules.
Why do we choose to hold on to some things in the Bible and
not others? This is a critical question that we must ask our-

4 See J. Kent Ashcroft, "An Open Letter to Dr. Laura," May, 2000. Although it
has been debated which came first, this letter was the source of a speech given in
an episode of the TV series, The West Wing.

selves. If the other laws no longer make sense, then why would the law on homosexuality?

And finally, Romans 1:26-27 states:

> For this reason God gave them up to degrading passions. Their women exchanged natural intercourse for unnatural, and in the same way also the men, giving up natural intercourse with women, were consumed with passion for one another. Men committed shameless acts with men and received in their own persons the due penalty for their error.

The problem with claiming that this text condemns homosexuality is that Paul is discussing something quite different. As John Boswell explains, Paul was not condemning a particular sexual behavior, but instead condemning the common infidelity of the Gentiles.[5] Paul was focused on men and women who were heterosexual, filled with lust, and seeking sexual relationships that were unnatural to them — especially prostitution with boys — which was a common practice. Sr. Margaret Farley explains that same-sex intercourse, especially among men, was commonplace as a result of Greek and Roman philosophy and culture. In fact, men were considered one another's intellectual equal and love and friendship among men was common. The only purpose of sex with women was to bear children.[6]

Paul does not discuss sexual orientation because there was no understanding of the concept at the time. He also does

5 John Boswell, *Christianity, Social Tolerance, and Homosexuality: Gay People in Western Europe from the Beginning of the Christian Era to the Fourteenth Century* (Chicago: Chicago University Press, 1980), 108.

6 Farley. *Just Love*, 17-56.

not discuss love or commitment within same-sex relationships. And finally, Paul also said it was unnatural for men to have long hair (1 Corinthians 11:14) and that women should be silent in church (1 Corinthians 14:34). So, I think it is reasonable to question what Paul had to say in the first place.

And while some people claim that the creation stories in Genesis (1-3) define marriage between a man and a woman; think again. First, most people do not even realize that there are two different creation stories written at two very different times. They present different stories with different intents. The first creation story was written by Jews exiled in Babylonia circa 500 B.C.E.; they adopted the Babylonian creation story and inserted the name Elohim, the Hebrew word for God. This allowed the Jews to keep their tradition alive while displaced in a foreign land. The second creation story written circa 900 B.C.E. tells the story of Adam and Eve and notes that woman is created as a partner for man to keep him from being lonely. These stories are considered myths — not false, but a literary form that tells a story to explain the unknown — written with the purpose of answering ultimate questions. Neither is about defining marriage.

If we got a nickel for every time we heard, "I have gay friends, I support their rights, I just don't think they should be able to get married," we could end global poverty. However, I find it necessary to point out that we are talking about a federal law in a secular nation; yet arguments against this law are based on Christian (mis)interpretations of the Bible. I am not saying that marriage equality should not exist within the Church - or any religion for that matter - far from it. Rather, when it comes to the political issue as it exists in the U.S. today, stances against marriage equality are based on religious belief rather than secular law. This in itself is hugely problematic.

So what would Jesus say about marriage equality? As I noted, Jesus does not speak about homosexuality. If it was an issue Jesus was concerned about, he surely would have said something. But Jesus is silent on this issue that has fueled a major debate in modern history in his name. Nevertheless, Jesus says many things that we could easily apply here: "love your neighbor," "do not judge," "welcome the stranger," "treat others as you would like to be treated." I could go on, but you get the picture.

We often fear what is different from us, and if we could get past our own intolerance and recognize the humanity of those who do not subscribe to normative hegemony, we might come to realize that we are all made in the image of God and that it is the character of our relationships that matters, not gender. According to Farley, "the key question is not whether same-sex relationships can be ethically justified, but what must characterize these relationships when they are justified...the justice ethic appropriate to heterosexual relationships is the same justice ethic appropriate to same-sex relationships."[7] No doubt, Farley bases her thoughts on the teachings of Jesus.

---

7 Ibid., 288.

Women's Rights

The Hobby Lobby decision that granted corporations the right to refuse coverage for birth control for women based on religious objections was a massive blow to women's human rights and reproductive justice. The government quickly responded by making contraception available to women at no cost through the Affordable Care Act. Nonetheless, as Cecile Richards, President of Planned Parenthood, argued,

> This accommodation shouldn't be necessary in the first place…A private company shouldn't be able to pick and choose what health care services they provide to their employees because they are women, LGBTQ, or any other class of people. The Supreme Court was wrong to allow companies to discriminate against their employees this way, and Congress needs to pass legislation to fix it.[1]

Sadly, women's human rights continue to be threatened in the Land of the Free. Inspired by Margaret Atwood's novel *The Handmaid's Tale*, women wearing white bonnets and long red cloaks are becoming a common occurrence throughout the nation. Aligning themselves with Atwood's argument that forced pregnancy is an act of slavery, these women are protesting new bills that are seeking to control further access to birth control and pregnancy termination. Most recently, the handmaids demonstrated in Missouri where a bill would allow employment and housing discrimination against individuals

---

1 Cecile Richards quoted in Kimberly Leonard, "After Hobby Lobby: A Way to Cover Birth Control," *U.S. News,* July 10, 2015. Retrieved from http://www.usnews.com/news/articles/2015/07/10/after-hobby-lobby-ruling-hhs-announces-birth-control-workaround.

who use contraception or seek pregnancy termination. "Blessed be the fruit."[2]

Women's issues are political in nature. As we move forward in time, it seems that social policy focused on issues that are connected to women and gender are taking a step backwards in the name of Christianity. Planned Parenthood and reproductive justice continue to be under attack, the pay gap remains intact, rape culture continues to be the norm, and parental leave and early childhood education continue to be considered women's issues rather than a concern for all in society.

Reproductive Justice

Planned Parenthood is continually demonized in the U.S. as a result of its practice of abortion. Yet, pregnancy termination constitutes only 3 percent of the services offered and no federal dollars can be used toward abortions except in the cases of rape, incest, and risk to the life of the mother per the Hyde Amendment. Defunding Planned Parenthood means leaving millions of women and men without access to cancer and STD screenings, contraception, and other women's health services. It is also an attack on the poor given that a very high percentage of those who use Planned Parenthood services fall into the low-income category. Politicians who boast of creating a "culture of life" by working toward defunding Planned Parenthood

---

2 Sejal Singh, "Missouri Votes to Let Employers Fire People Who Use Birth Control," *Feministing,* June 21, 2017. Retrieved from http://feministing. com/2017/06/21/missouri-votes-to-let-employers-fire-people-who-use-birth-control/.

seem to have a limited definition of life.

Abortion is a difficult issue; it is divisive and people on both sides often ignore the complexities that exist. Many people have created an image in their minds of who the woman is seeking an abortion: someone who takes no precautions, who exposes herself to risk, and who has abortions rather than using birth control. Such a claim is lazy and uninformed. Women seek abortions for a number of reasons and we give little thought to the suffering endured as a result. Likewise, we often don't hold men accountable for their role in pregnancy.

Yet, conservative political candidates argue that a woman's body is not her own and some claim that an abortion is never permissible, even in cases of rape, incest, and danger to the mother's life. Former presidential candidate Mike Huckabee argued that a ten year old girl should be denied an abortion after being raped by her stepfather. Is such a response really based on Christian teaching?

The fact is that no one is "pro-abortion." The language of "pro-choice" and "pro-life" is highly problematic and only fuels the fire of the debate. I choose to discuss reproductive justice, something for which I believe Planned Parenthood advocates. If we can look at the issues that exist as being related to social justice and recognize that this means much more than abortion, the conversation could shift. Sr. Joan Chittister has eloquently explained this saying,

I do not believe that just because you're opposed to

abortion, that that makes you pro-life. In fact, I think in many cases, your morality is deeply lacking if all you want is a child born but not a child fed, not a child educated, not a child housed. And why would I think that you don't? Because you don't want any tax money to go there. That's not pro-life. That's pro-birth. We need a much broader conversation on what the morality of pro-life is.[3]

Pope Francis called for a "Year of Mercy" and stated that if a woman confessed to having an abortion, she would be forgiven. Many have praised the pope for taking such a step towards healing; yet, I can't help but think, "how judgmental and irresponsible." Without knowing a woman's circumstance, her decision-making process, her doctor's concerns, etc., why should one be told to repent? I appreciate Pope Francis' great commitment to the poor and social justice. However, he has failed to recognize the deep interconnection between poverty and women's issues. To deny women the right to reproductive justice is to deny women the ability to make decisions about their physical, emotional, and financial health. So in the "Year of Mercy," I wonder whether the Vatican confessed its own sins against women, LGBTQIA persons, and others it has marginalized?

Many people argue that Jesus would never support abortion. Yet, I think Jesus would recognize the complexity of reproductive justice and how interconnected it is with other

---

3 Joan Chittister quoted in Leslie Salzillo, "Catholic Nun Explains Pro-Life in a Way that Will Stun Many (Especially Republican Lawmakers)," *The Daily Kos,* July 30, 2015. Retrieved from http://www.dailykos.com/story/2015/07/30/1407166/-Catholic-Nun-Explains-Pro-Life-In-A-Way-That-May-Stun-The-Masses.

oppressive structures including poverty, racism, and sexism. Given that his political stances focused on uprooting oppression and creating a community based on social justice, conversations on reproductive issues would, I think, be critical for Jesus.

Complementarity

The idea of complementarity upheld by Pope Francis also greatly contributes to economic injustice for women. According to this teaching, men and women have specific roles and are meant to complement each other. This is not a teaching of Jesus, but rather a teaching created by Pope John Paul II and implemented by the patriarchal structure of the Vatican. Such an idea argues that women are valued for their roles as wife and mother and has long been manifested and promoted within American political culture.

Complementarity is highly problematic in that it denies women's value in any other role. As a woman with an ongoing struggle with infertility, I find it troubling that my church sees me as less valuable because my womb is barren. Likewise, do women have less value if they choose a career over motherhood? What if they choose not to marry? There are also clear implications for single parents, LGBTQIA parents, and so on.

The Vatican's refusal to value women's roles outside the home influences social policy on women's issues. The continued struggle to close the pay gap, implement paid parental leave, create viable options for childcare and early childhood education are directly connected to complementarity. If women are supposed to remain in the home and be wives and mothers, then there is no need to address any of these issues. How can we possibly have women in leadership roles if they are supposed to be at home cooking dinner and caring for children? And so, when women do pursue careers, the social attitude is that women do not belong in the workforce. Such an idea is even more problematic for women of color with a lower pay rate and many who have historically worked outside of the home as a result of the intersection of gender, economic injustice, and racism. In this secular nation, Christian values dominate our political debates. And to be frank, these are community issues that impact men as well as women; yet they have been deemed women's issues because of particular theological teachings and social norms.

Rape Culture

The existence of rape culture and ongoing violence against women is also a community issue that affects all genders. We understand rape culture as one that normalizes violence against women, objectifies women's bodies, and disregards women's rights. Although generally connected to sexual assault, rape culture must be recognized as perpetuating widespread violence against women because of gender. Domestic violence continues to be a leading cause of death among women in the U.S. and while statistics claim that one in three women experiences sexual violence in their lifetimes, the number is much higher and cannot be accurately measured due to low reporting caused by the level of shame and blame perpetrated by society.

Religion, and Christianity specifically, contribute to this culture
as a result of sexist teachings developed by a patriarchal institution, of which complementarity is one. Again, our (mis)inter-
pretations of the Christian tradition as taught by Jesus results in
a culture that is abusive to women.

Susan Brownmiller began a conversation in 1975 with
her groundbreaking book *Against Our Will: Men, Women, and
Rape.*[4] She described the rape culture and called attention to the
double victimization endured by those who have been sexually assaulted. Sadly, little has changed in the last four decades.
Rape and sexual victimization are normalized, victims are
blamed, and society sympathizes with rapists.

You may recall what has become known as "Steubenville," the shocking gang rape of a teenage girl by two boys who
were considered football stars in the small town. As they assaulted the victim, bystanders took video and pictures tweeting
and sharing the brutal attack on Youtube — rape culture in the
world of social media. How bold and telling to think it reasonable to share rape with the world as if it should be applauded.
But then again, societal attitudes certainly support such disregard for women and girls while praising male dominance.

"Steubenville" made national news because many people
in the town blamed the victim and tried to protect the rapists
by recognizing them only as the athletes they needed to win
football games. Alas, high school football is valued over the

---

4 Susan Brownmiller, *Against Our Will: Men Women and Rape,* (New York:
Simon and Schuster, 1975).

lives of women and girls. Eventually the two boys were convicted and many were outraged with CNN reporters Poppy Harlow and Candice Crowley who sympathized with the rapists, lamenting that their lives were ruined.[5] What about the victim? I have to wonder when there will be the acknowledgement and prosecution of hate crimes against women?

The Women's March

The day after Trump's inauguration, women, men, and children took to the streets around the world to demand legislation and social policy that protect women's human rights. The violent rhetoric of the election cycle led to anger, fear, and a division of the nation. The thought that the American people could elect a man to office who denigrated and demonized so many people and who openly admitted to sexually assaulting women is devastating. Women developed the Women's March in response to the election. It has continued to be a source of strength, and has led to many people taking action and voicing their resistance to such treatment of women. While this movement clearly focuses on issues related to women, the March also focuses on racism, heterosexism, and xenophobia. Recognizing the issue of intersectionality, that every type of oppression is intertwined, and that one form of oppression cannot be uprooted alone, the Women's March is rightly working toward uprooting all oppressions.

---

5 Erik Wemple, "CNN is Getting Hammered for Steubenville Coverage," *The Washington Post*, March 18, 2013. Retrieved from https://www.washingtonpost.com/blogs/erik-wemple/wp/2013/03/18/cnn-is-getting-hammered-for-steubenville-coverage/.

The movement's guiding principles focus on nonvio-
lence, unity, working within the community, and addressing
violent acts rather than attacking people. And note here the
meaning of violence - not only physical injury, but any act that
seeks to harm a person including emotional, psychological, and
spiritual abuse. Abuse is the act of claiming power over others
and seeking to subjugate someone for the sake of one's own
privilege. Oppression and marginalization are acts of violence
and they were continually perpetrated against the disenfranchised throughout the election cycle.

In response to the Women's March, many religious wom-
en protested that their participation was not welcomed. Why?
In light of its feminist stance on reproductive rights, the Wom-
en's March rejected partnerships with pro-life organizations.
Organizers explained that all were welcome to participate, but
that it was not the time or the place to protest abortion. Instead
the March and the overall movement was focused on securing
women's human rights of which reproductive rights is considered to be one aspect of. To use the March as a platform to
protest abortion would interrupt the focus of the movement
and create division in the conversation around women's human
rights.

Some people have asked whether there is room for conservative feminists in the movement. While conservative and
feminism seems to be an oxymoron, it refers to women who
support women's rights on nearly all issues other than abortion.
And there certainly is room for these women in the movement.
Their voices should be heard about pay inequity, violence

against women, and so on. However, if conservative feminists cannot separate the issues and focus on those they support, then the message and mission of the March will no longer be the focus. Rather than progress we will only see dissension on this divisive issue. It will dominate the conversation and all other objectives will be lost.

Following the March on Washington and cities around the world, a second event was held on International Women's Day called Day Without a Woman. The goal was for women to take the day off to demonstrate how much everyone relies upon their talents and abilities are relied on. There were some issues with this given that many of the women the March is standing up for could not afford to miss a day of work. Nonetheless, thousands of women protested using the hashtag #daywithoutawoman.

There was a vehement backlash to the event and to feminism; a Twitter storm of virulent tweets with the hashtag #daywithoutafeminist mocked the women's strike.

- *Today is REALLY a #daywithoutafeminist REAL women work, take care of family & home, businesses, or at gun range!*[6]

- *March 8th isn't a #daywithoutawoman, it's a #daywithoutafeminist. Thank you, ladies, for giving us a day off from your insane bullshit.*[7]

---

6 Lori Hendry. Twitter Post. March 8, 2017, 8:34 AM. https://twitter.com/Lrihendry/status/839469265107439619.

7 Jessica. Twitter Post. March 8, 2017, 2:44 AM. https://twitter.com/associatedjess/status/839381322690936832.

- *It's #DayWithoutAFeminist & they don't realize how many are like "Wooo! This is great!" #DayWithoutAWoman*[8]

While both conservatives and progressives critiqued the event, Evangelical women saw it as an opportunity to voice their response to the feminist movement using social media. Still clinging to gender roles based on the ideas of complimentarily, submission to male headship, and biblical womanhood, antifeminist religious women argued that feminism not only goes against God, but also undermines women's ability to be active agents and control our own actions. According to this argument, feminists focus on gender as the problem rather than our individual decision making. By calling out sexism and demanding change, we neglect our own responsibilities. In turn, we are disempowering ourselves and become victims of our own bad behavior.[9]

This argument ignores the complexities that exist within sexist oppression. It disregards intersectionality, rape culture, and structural misogyny and such a claim is based on a privileged perspective that rests on the assumption of autonomy.[10] Women have varying levels of privilege; sexism and violence against women are experienced in different ways based on race, ethnicity, religion, and social position. Sarah and Hagar of the Bible continue to emulate the struggle of women based on privilege in society today. While Sarah is clearly oppressed as

8 Jude Eden. Twitter Post. March 8, 2017, 4:22 PM. https://twitter.com/Jude_Eden/status/839587212379451392.

9 See Kira Ganga Kieffer. "Why I Didn't March for You: How Evangelicals are Reframing Antifeminism Post-Trump." FSR Forum. March 23, 2017. Retrieved from http://www.fsrinc.org/blog/why-i-didnt-march-for-you/.

10 Ibid.

a woman whose only purpose is to give birth, she has far more privilege than her handmaid, Hagar who is forced into slavery and to give birth to a child Sarah claims as her own, and is then driven into the wilderness.

While we are all active agents in our lives, survival means different actions for different women depending on her life circumstances. To claim that feminists are victims of their own ideas and actions is to disempower and reinforce patriarchal structures that implement misogyny.

When considering Jesus' teachings, I think it is fair to say that Jesus was a feminist. While there are many different definitions of feminism, all draw from a basic foundational understanding. Rosemary Radford Ruether[11] and bell hooks[12] help us to recognize these core philosophies through their writings. Feminism calls for honoring the full humanity of all women and all men. It also calls us to recognize intersectionality and how it impacts one's experience of oppression. As hooks notes, equity and justice will not result from the feminist revolution; rather we must also end racism, imperialism, class elitism, and all oppressions so that every person can become "fully self-actualized" women and men and so that mutuality shapes our interactions. We do that so we can live together in loving and just communities.[13] Doesn't this sound like what Jesus called for

---

11 Rosemary Radford Ruether "What is Feminism?" *Feminism and Religion*. Retrieved from https://feminismandreligion.com/rosemary-radford-ruether-on-feminism/.

12 bell hooks, *Feminism is for Everyone* (Cambridge, MA: South End Press, 2000).

13 Ibid.

all along?

Jesus on Women

Many people claim the Bible and the lack of women in Jesus' ministry as evidence of women's subordinate position in society. They rely upon teachings like complementarity to justify women's roles and reinforce social norms that keep women from being recognized as fully human. Nonetheless, women played a critical role in Jesus' ministry. Jesus had women disciples, of whom Mary Magdalene was one. That's right, not a prostitute, a disciple. And, women were priests in the Catholic Church for the first thousand years as papal letters and inscriptions demonstrate.[14]

The Gospels show that Jesus repeatedly broke cultural norms when it came to engaging with women. Jewish culture was highly patriarchal and women's roles were limited to the home as wife, mother, and host. Women were not to be greeted in public by men and throughout their lives were always under the authority of a man — either their fathers or husbands. They had little access to inheritance or property. While men could divorce their wives for almost any reason, women were not permitted to divorce their husbands. The interior of synagogues were divided by gender with women being restricted to an outer court and refused the right to pray aloud. Thus, women were a highly vulnerable population — something Jesus recognized and to which he responded by defying cultural norms in several

---

14 See Karen Jo Torjesen, When Women Were Priests. (New York: Harper Collins, 1993).

ways.

To begin with, Jesus treats women with dignity and often spoke with women in public. He spoke with the widow at Nain whose only son had died. Having compassion for her, Jesus told her not to weep and raised her son from the dead (Luke 7: 11-17). He also healed a woman who had been crippled for eighteen years calling her "daughter of Abraham" (Luke 13:16)[15] and had a long conversation with a Samaritan woman who went on to testify on his behalf (John 4:9, 27).

Although women were deemed ritually unclean during menstruation, Jesus healed a woman who had been isolated for twelve years due to unceasing blood flow. The woman had touched his cloak; rather than becoming angry because custom dictated that such an act rendered Jesus unclean, Jesus called the woman "daughter" and told her that her faith had healed her (Luke 8:48). He also refused to judge women who were considered sinful. Jesus allowed himself to be anointed by a woman whom society judged harshly (Luke 7:36-50), and also by a woman who was an adulterer (John 8:3-11).

Jesus not only had women disciples, but also selected women as prominent recipients of his revelation. Jesus reveals himself as the Messiah to the Samaritan woman and told Martha, sister of Lazarus, that he is "the resurrection and the life" (John 11:25). Most notably, Jesus chose women as the first

---

15 Note that although men were referred to respectfully as "sons of Abraham," no such reference existed for women. Thus, Jesus calling the crippled woman "daughter of Abraham" was a clear sign of dignity and Jesus' acknowledgement of the woman's equal worth to men.

witnesses of his resurrection. While the apostles did not believe Mary Magdalene's testimony, nevertheless she persisted. Without her witness, Christianity would not exist today.

Jesus' message was overwhelmingly focused on love, inclusion, social justice, and liberation for all — including women. Our society has used ideas like complementarity to create substructures to marginalize women. These are not teachings from Jesus and are not ordained by God, but rather are man-made structures that support an ongoing power dynamic that keeps women from being recognized as fully human. Like as any oppressive structure, this is in direct conflict with the teachings of the Gospel.

Capital Punishment

Republican Governor of Arkansas Asa Hutchinson attempted to carry out an unprecedented eight executions in eleven days in April, 2017. Sr. Helen Prejean, known for her anti-capital punishment stance, challenged Hutchinson saying, "Governor, be a statesman and a real moral leader of the people…Do what is morally right. As a state official, you should not be involved in the deliberate killing of human beings."[1] Nonetheless, Hutchinson prevailed with four executions; the additional four death row inmates received last minute stays.

While Hutchinson received much criticism from advocates against capital punishment, there are some executions that have been widely supported. For instance, Timothy McVeigh, who planned the Oklahoma City Murrah Federal Building bombing, was put to death on June 11, 2001, an execution that was supported by 80 percent of Americans. Including ninetenn children, 168 people were killed in that terrorist attack. One can only imagine how the relatives of those victims felt. These family members were divided on the issue of capital punishment, but many supported McVeigh's execution. Some awaited his death with anticipation, while others became outspoken opponents of the death penalty. And some families were split. For instance, Tom and Marsha Knight, who lost their daughter in the bombing, had totally different stances on the issue. While Mrs. Knight felt that viewing the McVeigh's execution would be

---

1 Sr. Helen Prejean quoted in Ed Pilkington, "Arkansas executions bring Sister Helen Prejean's death penalty fight to the fore," *The Guardian*, April 21, 2017.

mentally unhealthy, her husband thought being a witness would offer him peace.[2]

Bud Welch, who lost his daughter, Julie-Marie, in the bombing commented that that he views the death penalty as "vengeance," something that does not promote the healing process. "Of course our first reaction is to strike back. But if we permit ourselves to think through our feelings, we might get to a different place. I was taught that even the souls of the dastardly criminals should be saved. I think it is necessary, even for the soul of Timothy McVeigh. I think my daughter's position would be the same as mine."[3]

I would like to think that I would have Welch's strength and conviction if I lost a loved one to violence, that I would maintain my anti-capital punishment stance; but the truth is that I don't know. Nonetheless, the question remains, can an execution provide what is needed to heal from such a tragedy? Can anything?

Jesus stood against capital punishment, and is the greatest example of the death penalty gone wrong. Many people cite the biblical verse "an eye for an eye" (Exodus 21:24) in an attempt to claim that God ordains executions. However, in doing so, they have ignored Jesus' teaching:

> You have heard that it was said, "An eye for an eye and a tooth for a tooth." But I say to you, Do not resist an evil-

---

2 Lois Romano and Dan Eggen, "For McVeigh's Victims, Different Paths to Peace," *The Washington Post*, April 15, 2001.

3 Bud Welch, "A Father's Urge to Forgive," *Time Magazine*, June 16, 1997.

doer. But if anyone strikes you on the right cheek, turn the other also; and if anyone wants to sue you and take your coat, give your cloak as well; and if anyone forces you to go one mile, go also the second mile. Give to everyone who begs from you, and do not refuse anyone who wants to borrow from you (Matt 5:38-42).

Statistics show that only 5 percent of Americans believe that Jesus would support government sanctioned executions (8 percent of Protestants, 2 percent of Catholics, and 10 percent of all practicing Christians); yet many nonetheless support the death penalty. A Barna poll shows that 38 percent of all Americans and 40 percent of Christians are in favor of capital punishment.[4]

Although capital punishment has proven not to be a deterrent[5] and is far more costly than alternative sentences,[6] it is legal in states throughout the U.S. In all, 141 countries have abolished the death penalty, and the majority of executions in the last decade have taken place in five countries: China, Iran, Yemen, North Korea, and the U.S. Only 2 percent of U.S. counties are responsible for the majority of executions in the nation; and it seems that the death penalty belt is the same as the Bible belt. As Prejean points out, "The real practitioners of death have always been the 10 southern states that practiced slavery, Arkansas among them."[7] Sixty-two U.S. counties are responsible

---

4 J. Merritt, "Poll: Younger Christians less supportive of death penalty," *Religion News Service,* January 18, 2014.

5 Max Ehrenfreund, "There's Still No Evidence that Executions Deter Crime," *The Washington Post,* April 30, 2014.

6 Maurice Chammah, "Six Reasons the Death Penalty is Becoming More Expensive," *The Marshall Project,* December 17, 2014.

7 Prejean quoted in Pilkington.

for the majority of executions since 1976 when the Supreme Court reinstated capital punishment. Eighty-five percent of the remaining 3081 counties have not carried out a death penalty sentence in over forty-five years.

The top ten counties within the 2 percent include:

- Harris County, Texas
- Dallas County, Texas
- Oklahoma County, Oklahoma
- Tarrant County, Texas
- Bexar County, Texas
- Montgomery County, Texas
- Tulsa County, Oklahoma
- Jefferson County, Texas
- St. Louis County, Missouri
- Brazos County, Texas

Recognizing the pockets where capital punishment is most practiced and the microcosms that exist in those areas reveals a great deal. Although Caucasians and African Americans are murdered at approximately the same rate, 80 percent of imposed death sentences are in cases where the victim is white. Likewise, African American defendants are twice as likely to be sentenced to death compared to white defendants. Ninety-eight percent of chief district attorneys in states that practice capital punishment are white and 1 percent is African American. In Texas, where most executions take place, only one white defendant who murdered an African American victim has been put to death since 1976.[8] In short, racism is a critical factor in the

---

8 See "The Baldus Study," David C. Baldus, George Woodworth, and Charles A. Pulaski, Jr., *Equal Justice and the Death Penalty: A Legal and Empirical Analysis,* (Boston: Northeastern University Press, 1990).

way capital punishment is imposed. While some people claim it is an appropriate response to heinous crimes and that it brings peace to families who have been victimized, it is simply another system used to continue the cycle of racism — and a very effective one at that. According to Martin O'Malley, "Our nation's legacy of slavery and racial injustice finds continued offense in our use of the death penalty. Our death row population is more than 40 percent black — nearly three times the proportion of the general population."[9]

Jesus calls us to be compassionate, merciful, and loving. Moreover, he calls us to dismantle systems of oppression. Capital punishment is just that — a complex system of oppression that continues a history of racism that is perpetuated through state sanctioned executions. There is no doubt that this is an emotional issue; particularly for those who have been affected by violent crime and seek retribution and healing. Nonetheless, while many people connect the death penalty to biblical justice, it is not supported by the Christian tradition.

According to Joseph Brennan, "Those whom we would banish from society or from the human community itself often speak in too faint a voice to be heard above society's demand for punishment. It is the particular role of courts to hear these voices, for the Constitution declares that the majoritarian chorus may not alone dictate the conditions of social life."[10] Jesus would agree with this statement.

9 Martin O'Malley, "Why the Death Penalty Needs to Go," *CNN.* November 6, 2015. Retrieved from http://www.cnn.com/2015/11/06/opinions/omalley-capital-punishment.

10 McCleskey v. Kemp, 481 U.S. 279, 343 (1987) (J. Brennan, dissenting).

#BlackLivesMatter

#BlackLivesMatter (BLM) was founded in 2012 following the murder of Trayvon Martin at the hands of George Zimmerman.[1] Martin's death highlighted the ongoing racial injustice and bigotry that continues to plague the U.S. and led to a response that calls for "broadening the conversation around state violence to include all of the ways in which Black people are intentionally left powerless at the hands of the state."[2]

Following Martin's murder, the killing of innocent African American men at the hands of police has persisted across the nation. Social media has become a platform to share videos of police shootings and executions, and these have fueled anger and demands for justice. At the same time, it has also resulted in the counter movements #AllLivesMatter and #BlueLivesMatter.

Some people have claimed that a Christian response to BLM is focusing on the idea that all lives matter, that God loves all people. While of course every life matters, such a response has once again claimed power and worked to silence the oppressed. Systemic and institutional racism are defining civil rights and social justice issues. To be silent about the injustice against African Americans is to be complicit in it. To respond with All Lives Matter is to perpetrate violence and once again

---

1 Zimmerman was eventually acquitted of murder and later sold the gun he used to kill Martin for over $120,000.

2 "About the #BlackLivesMatter Network." #BlackLivesMatter. Retrieved from http://blacklivesmatter.com/about/.

silence those who have been historically disenfranchised.

Tomi Lahren, formerly of The Blaze, has highly criticized BLM publicly calling it "the new KKK" and a "militant and overtly aggressive"[3] movement that seeks to attack whites and police. According to Lahren, BLM moved from protesting to "rioting, looting, and burning, and militant action." Referring to the protest in Dallas, she argued that BLM was responsible for five fallen officers — certainly tragic. However, as Trevor Noah pointed out during their interview, anyone can commit a violent act in the name of any movement. That does not mean that is what the movement represents. Interestingly, Lahren argued that while some officers have committed bad acts, such acts cannot be used to judge all police officers. Nonetheless, she has failed to recognize the same logic when it comes to BLM.[4]

When it comes to law enforcement and the criminal justice system, American Americans and Caucasian Americans have significantly different experiences. And thus, we have a moral obligation to stand in solidarity with our African American brothers and sisters. This is not to say that the lives of police officers do not matter or are not valued. Their commitment and sacrifice to our communities must be appreciated and respected. However, it is clear that our justice system is not color blind and that equitable justice under the law does not exist.

---

3 Tomi Lahren Interview. *The Daily Show with Trevor Noah. Comedy Central.* New York, December 1, 2016. Television.
4 Ibid.

It is not the individual police officers who are to blame; rather this is a systemic issue that pervades our society. It is interwoven into our institutions and marginalizes persons of color. This is not about the bad acts of a few police officers or the discrimination that can occur between individuals. So BLM is a justified and appropriate response to institutional and systemic violence that continually oppresses.

Following Trump's election to the White House, Dave Chappell appeared on Saturday Night Live. He took on the criticism of BLM and the All Lives Matter and Blue Lives Matter responses. Chappell asks, "Why do we have to say black lives matter?" He goes on to say it is a catchy slogan because everyone else seems to be claiming it, like Blue Lives Matter. "What? Were you born a police? That is not a blue life, that's a blue suit. If you don't like it take that suit off and find a new job, because I'm gonna tell you right now. If I could quit being black today, I'd be outta the game."[5] As he delivered his monologue, crowds roared with laughter; but the poignancy of his words remains.

Racism is "America's original sin."[6] Our nation was founded on the backs of slaves. The history of the kidnapping and enslavement of Africans in the "New World" resulted in the subsequent discrimination of African Americans upheld by ongoing systemic violence. As Wallis explains, "one would think that national repentance and reparations would be called

5 Dave Chappell, "Monologue," *Saturday Night Live, NBC*, New York. November 13, 2016. Television.

6 See Jim Wallis, *God's Politics: Why the Right Gets it Wrong and the Left Doesn't Get it* (New York: HarperSanFrancisco, 2005); and Jim Wallis, *American's Original Sin: Racism, White Privilege, and the Bridge to a New America* (Grand Rapids, MI: Brazos Press, 2017).

for. But neither has ever come. Even apologizing for this great sin has proved to be quite controversial."[7] Interestingly, the U.S. has made public apologies in the past including those to Japanese Americans for internment camps during WWII and to native Hawaiians for participating in the overthrowing of the Kingdom of Hawaii. Nonetheless, a public apology acknowledging the injustice and consequences of slavery — tearing apart families, torturing, and murdering human beings because of their race — has not occurred.

The murders of Trayvon Martin, Freddie Gray, Michael Brown, Walter Scott, Alton Sterling, Philandro Castile, Tamir Rice, and so many more, as well as the death of Sandra Bland, are evidence of the critical race issues and violation of human rights for African Americans that continue in the U.S. Black Lives Matter is a response to the indignity of a nation that was founded on slavery and has never created an opportunity for healing. While some people claim that an apology for slavery is unwarranted, it would begin the restorative process. Restitution is necessary. Without it, systemic violence will be reinforced and injustice will prevail. Xochitl Alvizo explains,

> Oppression is systemic. Injustice is systemic. It pervades the whole – it seeps into everyday actions and becomes habits and patterns that function as default. As a result, the actions that fall within these patterns hardly need justifying. If anything, the questioning of them is what is put on the defensive. And those who stand against injustice must usually do so in the face of militarized policing, before vast forces that serve to preserve the

---

7 Wallis, *God's Politics*, 308.

status quo.[8]

According to Alvizo, an act of systemic violence should not be an occasion for remembering the victim with "reflection and understanding." Rather, it should prompt us to recognize that such violence impacts us all; it calls us to anger — righteous anger. Beverly Harrison tells us that "Anger is — and it always is — a sign of some resistance in ourselves to the moral quality of the social relations in which we are immersed."[9] Anger tells us there is injustice; indeed there is injustice. As Martin Luther King Jr. stated, "Injustice anywhere is a threat to justice everywhere. We are caught in an inescapable network of mutuality, tied in a single garment of destiny."[10]

Change only occurs when we are willing to listen to one another, truly to hear the struggles and grievances of our neighbors. It is true: all lives do matter. However, all lives won't matter until Black lives matter too.

---

8 Xochitl Alvizo.,"The Systemic Killing of Michael Brown," *Feminism and Religion*, August 14, 2014. Retrieved from https://feminismandreligion. com/2014/08/14/systemic-violence-and-the-killing-of-michael-brown-by-xochitl-alvizo/.

9 Beverly Harris, "The Power of Anger in the Work of Love," in Ann Loads (ed.) *Feminist Theology: A Reader*, (Louisville, KY: Westminster John Knox Press1990), 206, cited in Alvizo, "The Systemic Killing of Michael Brown."

10 Martin Luther King Jr., "Letter from Birmingham City Jail," in James Melvin Washington (ed.) *A Testament of Hope: The Essential Writings of Martin Luther King Jr.* (New York: New American Library, 1982), 290.

Climate Change

The Paris Agreement or the Paris Climate Accord was one of Barack Obama's defining achievements during his eight years in office. In all, 195 nations signed the thirty-one-page document to mark their commitment to work together to reduce global warming. Following the signing of the agreement Obama said "Together, we've shown what's possible when the world stands as one."[1]

Shortly after Trump took office, he pulled the U.S. out of the Agreement; after all, he has claimed that global warming is a Chinese hoax. He has also tweeted 115 times about his skepticism of climate change. According to Trump, it was cold and snowing in New York in October; thus there is no such thing as global warming. Perhaps someone should tell him it is about shifting weather patterns because of the warming of the planet, not simply warm weather.

While ninety-seven percent of scientists agree that global warming is real, it continues to be an issue that divides the left and the right. Democrats argue that we are facing a grave threat and must reduce carbon emissions before it is too late. Republicans continue either to refuse to acknowledge the issue or claim it has nothing to do with human action.

Climate change is the greatest threat to humanity. As

1 Barack Obama, "Statement by the President on the Paris Climate Agreement." December 12, 2015. Retrieved from https://obamawhitehouse.archives.gov/the-press-office/2015/12/12/statement-president-paris-climate-agreement.

Obama noted, to refuse to act is to condemn our children to a planet that is irreparable.[2] Since the late nineteenth century, the Earth has warmed about two degrees Fahrenheit. Emissions have soared in modern times, and physics tells us that adding carbon dioxide - as well as other greenhouse gases - to the atmosphere traps extra heat near the surface of the planet. Such an understanding demonstrates that human action is at fault for climate change.

Although some people continue to argue that natural forces are responsible for global warming, scientists have ruled out such an explanation and have time and again stated that human action — without a doubt — is the cause.

So why the argument? It's quite simple. Big money - or "dark money" as Jane Mayer calls it.[3] The Citizens United Supreme Court Decision in 2010 allows corporations and unions to spend unlimited funds to influence the political process. You may have heard of the Koch brothers, billionaires who made their fortune through fossil fuel. They own oil refineries in several states and control approximately four thousand miles of pipeline. They also own products like Dixie cups and Brawny paper towels. Koch Industries is the second-largest private company in America.

The Koch brothers are American made oligarchs who support libertarian values, particularly minimal social services for the poor, reduced taxes for corporations, and less industry

2 Ibid.
3 Jane Mayer, *Dark Money: The Hidden History of the Billionaires Behind the Rise of the Radical Right* (New York: First Anchor Books, 2016).

oversight, especially for environmental regulations. You see, Koch Industries ranks among the top three polluters of water, air, and climate in the U.S., and generates twenty-four million metric tons of greenhouse gases each year. They've also been fined record penalties due to their environmental violations and the largest wrongful death judgment in American history as a result of one of their pipelines exploding and incinerating two teenagers in Texas.

Nonetheless, with $80 billion at their disposal, the Koch brothers continue to violate environmental regulations and use their fortune to control Republican politicians - particularly on climate change. It is the Koch brothers who are funding Republican campaigns and influencing the political terrain to ensure that the GOP wins Senate seats. Without the Koch brothers' money, many Republicans would be out of office; the Koch brothers are buying their votes on climate policy.

With an insatiable appetite for power, money, and control, the Koch brothers are manipulating the political process from behind the scenes with no care for the destruction they are leaving behind. They continue to try to buy both Congress and the White House without apology, and their financial influence keeps our nation from moving forward on climate change policy.

Before Trump was elected president, he was already in bed with the fossil fuel industry. The Washington Post reported that "the fossil fuel industry is enjoying a remarkable resurgence as its executives and lobbyists shape President-elect

Donald Trump's policy agenda and staff his administration."[4]

Such influence is easily recognizable in Trump's appointment of Scott Pruitt to head up the Environmental Protection Agency (EPA), and Rex Tillerson, the former CEO of Exxon-Mobil, as Secretary of State. Pruitt has been a long time ally of the fossil fuel industry and sued the EPA fourteen times during his tenure as Oklahoma's Attorney General. To say the Trump Administration's connection to the fossil fuel industry runs deep is a gross understatement.

In March 2017 Trump signed an executive order that overturned Obama's Clean Power Plan. He has also proposed cutting the EPA budget by one-third and eliminating carbon research programs. With Trump's decision to back out of the Paris Climate Accord, the U.S. has become one of only three nations not involved in the agreement - the others being Nicaragua and Syria.

With fewer than one hundred days under his belt as POTUS, Trump ensured that combating climate change would be set back for quite some time. While the rest of the world is working towards ending global warming, Trump, the Koch brothers, and the Republican Party are pulling in the other direction.

---

4 Juliet Eilperin, Steven Mufson, and Philip Rucker, "The Oil and Gas Industry is Quickly Amassing Power in Trump's Washington," *The Washington Post*, December 14, 2016. Retrieved from https://www.washingtonpost.com/politics/the-oil-and-gas-industry-is-quickly-amassing-power-in-trumps-washington/2016/12/14/0d4b26e2-c21c-11e6-9578-0054287507db_story.html?utm_term=.ee14410ac5b6.

It's true that global warming was not an issue during Jesus' time. But big money manipulating the system so it can become more powerful without concern for the welfare of others sounds a lot like the politics against which Jesus stood. We should all be outraged that the future of our planet and the well-being of the generations to come rest on the selfishness of a few billionaires and the willingness of some politicians to acquiesce to benefit their careers.

Following Trump's withdrawal from the Paris Accord, Erick Erickson tweeted "I worship Jesus, not Mother Earth. He calls us to be good stewards of the planet, but that doesn't mean I have to care about global warming."[5] Although he contradicts himself, Erickson is one of the many conservative Christians who believe in dominion theology, the idea that God gave a biblical mandate for humans to rule over the Earth, and that we thus bear no responsibility for its destruction. The fossil fuel industry, and those who run it, have successfully used this ideal to manipulate the Religious Right into helping them cash in while life-giving resources perish.

Eco-justice is a Christian value. We must care for the Earth — God's creation — so that it can continue to sustain the world. And that means combatting climate change. In June 2015 Pope Francis released a 190-page statement on the environment that calls us to care for our common home. It was the first time that the world's largest religious body had developed a detailed statement advocating for the welfare of the planet.

---

5 Erick Erickson. Twitter Post. May 31, 2017. 4:26pm. https://twitter.com/EWErickson/status/870013673753919488.

Whereas encyclicals in the past were written to bishops, and then Catholics in general, this particular statement was addressed to all of humanity. According to the pope, global warming is a sin against creation, and it is the work of mercy to protect the planet.

Francis, who chose his name in honor of the thirteenth century friar recognized as the patron saint of the poor, animals, and the environment, explained that his experience in Latin America inspired him to write the document. It is the Global South and the poor that suffer the most as a result of climate change. Those who depend on the land for survival are in constant danger of droughts, rising sea levels, and devastating storms.

Although Pope Francis has stated that his encyclical is a theological and not a political statement, given his global popularity and timing he has clearly influenced the debate. Francis says explicitly that it is economic development and human action that has caused climate change, and describes this as man having "slapped nature in the face." Through global capitalism, unsustainable consumption, and greed we have exploited the environment and constructed vast inequalities and injustice.

To say that Jesus wouldn't care about global warming is to say that he would not care about the exploitation of the poor and God's creation. Understanding Jesus' politics and his focus on community, compassion, and the oppressed tells us where he would stand on this issue. Climate change would be at the top of Jesus' agenda.

Conclusion

When it comes down to it, both Democrats and Republicans get it wrong. While Democratic positions more closely mirror the ideas of social justice presented by Jesus, today's politicians come to the issues from problematic perspectives. For Jesus, the question is "how can we achieve common good for every person?" Politics today is so wrapped up in bureaucracy that the purpose of having a government gets lost. Rather than emphasizing the needs of the people, some politicians are focused on the game; they put up borders and refuse to work across the aisle for fear that their side will lose.

We are in the midst of one of the greatest financial, social, and political crises of our history and the attitudes of our politicians contribute to this greatly. When can we move beyond taking sides and work for positive change? This is what Jesus would want to know. For him, government should not function in any other way. Jesus' social policy would demand that people be at the center and every act focus on supporting humanity.

Jesus in the White House

Everyone with political responsibility
should remember two things: human
dignity and the common good.
- Pope Francis

While many people have been very troubled by Donald Trump's candidacy and eventual election to the highest office in the nation – and the world – 81 percent of Evangelicals and 65 percent of Catholics gave their vote to Trump. Given that social justice is a Christian tradition – not a liberal agenda as so many have claimed – such statistics are more than surprising. Although his campaign was based on silencing the disenfranchised and reclaiming power for the privileged, those who claim to be followers of Jesus still chose Trump as their candidate.

Given the mission of Jesus, the question is why so many

who claim to follow his teachings would participate in the election of a man who has repeatedly proven to be racist, sexist, xenophobic, cruel, and shows such disregard for creation. What part of the Christian tradition would condone such a vote?

While some people have claimed that Trump was the appropriate candidate because of his "pro-life" stance, Trump's rhetoric and actions toward people and planet clearly demonstrate he is "anti-life."

Although I would like to believe that such ignorance played a role in every Trump vote, the bottom line is that many people agree with his hateful rhetoric and actions and seek a nation that will continue to privilege some while oppressing others. Giving up privilege feels like marginalization; however until that happens injustice will continue for the historically disenfranchised. Hence, if Jesus were to run for POTUS, we can be pretty certain he wouldn't get the Christian vote. Nonetheless, it is reasonable to wonder how a Jesus Administration would differ from the current Trump Administration.

The Trump Administration

Within the first few weeks of Trump's presidency, he was referred to as "batshit crazy" by a Republican lawmaker.[1] While it was clear that Trump wanted to win the presidency, once he took office, he seemed to be surprised that he actually had to govern and work with Congress, for as a business mogul Trump

1 Maeve Reston, "Inside Trump's Tumultuous First 100 Days," *CNN.com.* Retrieved from http://www.cnn.com/interactive/2017/politics/state/inside-donald-trumps-tumultuous-first-100-days.

has been used to being in full control. He seems unsure of how to govern or enact policy changes that benefit the nation rather than himself and his business interests. Trump has repeatedly attempted to repeal acts without having a viable plan to replace them and seems to be trying to check off boxes rather than make real change.

His narcissism may be his greatest downfall. "Trump is so concerned about an image he can't control and staffers are so anxious about their standing with him that the administration easily slides into dysfunction."[2] Following his speech lambasting "American carnage," one of his very first acts as president was to demand that additional photos be released showing a larger crowd at his inauguration. While more than a million Americans participated in the Women's March the day after the inauguration (a crowd much larger than the one for the inaugurataion) and millions more did so around the world, Press Secretary Sean Spicer stood before correspondents and claimed that Trump had the largest presidential inauguration audience ever.

Trump's incessant tweeting for attention continually undercuts members of his administration and party. And his focus on "alternative facts" and "fake news" has dominated the media cycle, said John Oliver, in the same way that "a fart dominates the interior of a Volkswagen Beetle...there is simply no escape from him."[3]

---

2 Ibid.

3 John Oliver, Episode 91, *Last Week Tonight, HBO*, New York, February 19, 2017. Television.

Shortly before leaving office, Obama took measures to block construction of the Dakota access pipeline, recognizing its danger to the environment and violation of the National Preservation Historic Act. As the Standing Rock Sioux Tribe stated in its lawsuit against the U.S. Army Corp of Engineers, "There is a high risk that culturally and historically significant sites will be damaged or destroyed in the absence of an injunction."[4] Regardless of these concerns, just four days into his presidency, Trump signed an executive order to advance the pipeline's approval in an effort to support Republican objectives to promote fossil fuel interests.

Seven days into his presidency, Trump signed an executive order banning citizens from seven predominantly Muslim nations from entering the U.S. In addition to his fanatical vetting plan to block "radical Islamic terrorists" from entering the U.S., Trump also established a religious test to be administered to refugees from Islamic nations. Christians and other religious adherents were to be granted priority over Muslims. Interestingly, none of the countries from which the 9/11 terrorists traveled were on the list.

There was immediate backlash from human rights activists who argued that the order was religious persecution, and the American Civil Liberties Union called it "a euphemism for discriminating against Muslims." The President of Oxfam America, Raymond C. Offenheiser, explained that "The refugees impacted by today's decision are among the world's most

---

4 Quoted in Rebecca Hersher, "Key Moments in the Dakota Access Pipeline Fight," *NPR, 90.3 WCPN Ideastream*, February 22, 2017. Radio.

vulnerable people — women, children, and men — who are simply trying to find a safe place to live after fleeing unfathomable violence and loss."[5]

Apparently, Trump had not read the part of the Constitution on equal protection rights and religious freedom. Federal courts immediately pushed back and blocked the order. When Trump attempted to revise the ban, it was again blocked. Such discrimination is not an American value, nor is it legal.

Trump then turned his attention to Obama, attacking him via his favorite form of communication, Twitter. He claimed that Obama had wiretapped his phones at Trump Tower based on an article written several months earlier that implied something different. Rather than checking the facts first, Trump had his usual knee-jerk reaction and immediately tweeted his rant. Remember, this is the person we are entrusting with the nuclear access codes.

His next action was to begin the repeal of the Affordable Care Act. Interestingly, when Trump met with Australia's prime minister, he commented that Australia had a far better health care system than the U.S. Australia has universal healthcare; however, that was never Trump's plan for a new healthcare act. In fact, he had no plan. While there had been much discussion around such an action throughout the presidential election season, Trump moved into the process with little thought and a debacle ensued. The GOP pulled legislation after fellow

---

5 Michael Shear and Helen Cooper, "Trump Bars Refugees and Citizens of Seven Muslim Countries," *The New York Times,* January 27, 2017.

Republicans revolted. Trump later commented, "nobody knew healthcare could be so complicated."[6] Really? Actually, everyone knew...except for him.

Throughout his campaign, Trump vowed to deport twelve million undocumented immigrants and he started that process shortly after being sworn in. Although he claimed the focus would begin with "bad hombres," instead we've seen immigrant arrests soar and families torn apart as mothers and fathers who have been in this country for decades, who have followed the rules, and worked hard to provide for their children have been snatched off the streets and detained until they were returned to their home countries. Likewise, the first protected DREAMer was deported. The impact has been devastating.

Trump's campaign promise to build a "Game of Thrones" sized wall to keep out "rapists and criminals" also became a focal point during his first weeks in office. Mexico made it very clear that it has no intention for paying for the wall's construction. In response, Trump withdrew his invitation to President of Mexico Enrique Pena Nieto to visit the White House, damaging another relationship with a U.S. ally. Although Trump campaigned on Mexico paying for the wall that would supposedly stop the transport of illegal drugs into the U.S., as Steve Chapman puts it, "Trump fooled a lot of voters when he made that promise, and he may have even fooled himself. But at some point, you run out of fools."[7]

---

6 Donald Trump quoted in Reston.

7 Steve Chapman, "Trump's Wall is Already Collapsing," *The Chicago Tribune,* March 31, 2017.

Nonetheless, Trump continues to move forward with plans for the wall and now claims that the U.S. will pay for it up front, but that Mexico will reimburse the U.S. So now, billions of dollars to construct a wall with bigoted intent is awaiting funding approval from Congress that will add to tax payers' costs. Incidentally, even if construction of the wall had begun on Trump's first day in office, it would likely not be completed by the end of his presidency. Immoral in itself, the wall is another failed campaign promise from Trump.

Then of course, there is North Korea, the Russia scandal, and Trump's inability to play nice with U.S. allies. His "bromance" with Vladimir Putin and back room dealings with Russia continue to dominate the headlines and Kim Jung Un continues to threaten to launch a nuclear bomb that will land on U.S. soil. Each of these issues need critical attention, although Trump is causing each to grow and become more catastrophic.

The Trump Presidency is nothing short of a disaster. While those who voted for him did so in hopes of having a president that would interrupt business as usual, Trump has rushed policies that are poorly planned, flagrant, and illegal. This is Trump's normal behavior. He has a record of reacting without thinking and is self-destructive. His tweets are damning evidence of that. Trump also thinks that being president means no one can hold him accountable; hence his firing of James Comey.[8] His first one hundred days concluded with the lowest approval rating of any president at that juncture dating

8 Although the White House had originally claimed it was because of Comey's poor handling of Hillary Clinton's emails, the next day Trump blatantly admitted it was because of the Russia investigation.

back to Eisenhower.

The Jesus Administration

Considering Jesus' stances on social policy, there is no doubt that a Jesus Administration would be radically different than our current administration. His focus on love, inclusion, liberation, and social justice would upend Trump's policies.

Jesus was anything but narcissistic. He committed his life to bettering the community and standing up against oppression at any cost. That last thing he would be concerned with is how large the crowd was at his inauguration. Unlike Trump, Jesus would enter the White House with a plan that is based on concerns related to social and economic justice. He would recognize how to implement those plans and engage with Congress based on the Constitution and his Commandments of love God and love your neighbor. His focus was and would be on working together for positive change.

Stepping into the Oval Office, Jesus' first intentions would not be to authorize the Dakota access pipeline, repeal health care, or ban refugees. Quite the opposite. Like the other "Big J.C." (Jimmy Carter), Jesus would seek to make government "competent and compassionate." Given his political stances, it is fair to assume that Jesus would recognize the devastating impact of the Dakota access pipeline on the people and the earth, that healthcare for every person would be a critical part of his economic justice plan, and that welcoming refugees — those who have been oppressed and deemed "the other" —

would be a priority.

A Jesus Administration would begin with two major objectives that are directly correlated: 1) economic justice, and 2) social justice.

Beginning with our current taxes, Jesus would remind us that "it is easier for a camel to fit through the eye of a needle than a rich man to enter the kingdom of God" (Matt 19:24). Currently there are exorbitant tax breaks for the wealthy, while struggling Americans are on payment plans with the government to meet their tax obligations. This doesn't sound all that different from the tax system of the first-century Roman Empire. Hence, Jesus would be intent on restructuring the current tax plan that requires higher contributions from the wealthy and far less from the other 99 percent.

Healthcare and fair wages would also be critical in a Jesus Administration. The Affordable Care Act was an important start in restructuring the existing health care system in this nation. But Jesus would take it a step further and work towards a universal health care plan acknowledging that it is a human right. Likewise, considering Jesus' response to the Roman Empire's efforts to commercialize and heavily tax the fishing industry, labor unions and a living wage would be high level agenda items under an economic justice plan.

Pope Francis has referred to capitalism as "terrorism against all of humanity" and Jesus would likely take a similar stance. Considering the human rights violations that take place around the world in order to produce goods that America consumes, Jesus would reiterate his focus on people, not things. He would recognize the role the U.S. plays in a globalized world and that American purchasing habits and wasteful tendencies directly impact the various injustices experienced around the globe. My guess is that he would have a copy of Eduardo Galeano's *Open Veins of Latin America* on his night stand and give serious consideration to the atrocities in which many Americans unknowingly participate.

The second part of Jesus' proposal would focus on the high level of social injustice in the U.S, which of course, is directly correlated to economic injustice. Issues like #BlackLivesMatter, reproductive justice, immigration, education, climate change, capital punishment, and ending war would be central in his plan. Jesus would be genuinely concerned about the state of our nation and recognize that systemic and institutional oppressions are cancers of our society. Welcoming refugees, supporting those in need, being hospitable, being non-judgmental, celebrating diversity, inclusivity, forgiveness, and having a community where every person has their needs met and is treated fairly, these are all part of Jesus' commandments: love God and love your neighbor as yourself. It seems we've lost sight of what these means; but precisely these should be our focus.

Jesus would have a tall order, and while it is questionable that even he could make such change possible, he would commit every resource he had to making it a reality. In its essence, his political action today would not differ from his political action in the first century.

Make Humanity Great Again

> Our role in life is to bring the light of our
> own souls to the dim places around us.
> - Joan Chittister

There is no doubt that our political system is failing and that people want change for good reason. Party politics have created a divide in our nation and we need to get back to focusing on the needs of the people rather than winning for "our side."

Donald J. Trump is not the answer to the issues the U.S. faces. With fewer than two hundred days in office he has encouraged an ongoing rift among citizens and has failed at everything. I know I've been hard on Trump, and I haven't been very Jesus-like as I've pointed out his flaws. However, he is making bad decisions from a position that is impacting every person in this nation, and around the globe. The presidency should be led with knowledge, grace, and compassion. Trump's bigotry, inexperience, and arrogance are at the very least troubling. Likewise, his refusal to learn and hid continued blatant lies threaten the nation and the safety of its people. The office of the presidency is a lot to carry on one's shoulders; gratifying one's ego is no reason to run for the highest office in the land.

Obviously, Jesus is not going to be in the White House. While Republicans continue to invoke his name, they need to stop co-opting Jesus' teachings with the intent of doing very un-Christian things. For the last forty years, the Christian Right has influenced American politics and it is time for the Religious Left to join the conversation. The morality of our society is at stake and the soul of our nation is being bought with "dark money." We are in danger of losing our humanity.

It is time for a serious response to the Christian Right. This ongoing movement has dominated our nation's political agenda and has led to the idea that Christianity and the GOP are synonymous. Studies demonstrate that many Americans are walking away from religion altogether because of the Christian Right's political influence.[1] It is time for us to recognize Christianity as more than a conservative movement seeking to high-jack policies and victimize the disenfranchised.

As citizens we are responsible for the future of our nation. Our responsibility begins with our vote. As Christian

1 Michael Lipka, "Why America's 'Nones' Left Religion Behind," *Pew Research*, August 24, 2016. Retrieved from http://www.pewresearch.org/fact-tank/2016/08/24/why-americas-nones-left-religion-behind/.

citizens we need to take our Christian identity seriously too. Religion does play a role in politics. Do we want to live out our faith, or do we cast our vote out of fear and anger?

Certainly we need to repair the rift and become one nation, a nation that is indivisible and promotes liberty and justice for all. Yet rather than sport the Trump slogan, "Make America Great Again," I urge you to engage in what is far more necessary. With an alt-right movement at its peak and institutional and systemic oppression continuing unchecked, follow the teachings of Jesus and "Make Humanity Great Again." It is far more necessary in this era.

Printed in Great Britain
by Amazon